Truly, God Is My Source

Truly, God Is My Source

SANDRA MURPHY

Made in Charleston, SC
www.PalmettoPublishingGroup.com

ISBN: 9781641117098

Scripture quotations marked (CEV) are taken from the Contemporary English Version © 1991, 1992, 1995 by American Bible Society, Used by Permission.

Scripture quotations marked CSB are been taken from the Christian Standard Bible®, Copyright © 2017 by Holman Bible Publishers. Used by permission. Christian Standard Bible•, and CSB® are federally registered trademarks of Holman Bible Publishers.

Scripture quotations marked (ESV) are taken from the ESV® Bible (The Holy Bible, English Standard Version®), copyright © 2001 by Crossway, a publishing ministry of Good News Publishers. Used by permission. All rights reserved."

Preface

God speaks to us, even today, in many ways. Anyone who wants to live, to be encouraged, and to grow in any area of their life will enjoy reading *"Truly God Is My Source"*. You see it is my belief that many of our modern-day self-improvement philosophies may actually be found in God's word.

Truly, God Is My Source is based on Isaiah 40:30-31 *Even youths will become weak and tired, and young men will fall in exhaustion. But those who trust in the LORD will find new strength. They will soar high on wings like eagles. They will run and not grow weary. They will walk and not faint. (NLT)*

Isaiah 40:30-31

Scriptures in this book speaks of love, hope, peace, joy, and strength. These scriptures were selected to encourage the reader to trust in God' strength to soar above life's trials. You will also find in this book a collection of inspirational affirmations, and simple prayers sent out initially via text messages to my millennial sons as words of encouragement. After sharing the messages with other family members and friends, I soon realized that these messages appealed to those of all ages, beliefs, and different walks of life.

The affirmations and prayers that accompany the scriptures are written in the first person, so that they may be more relatable the reader. Scriptures, from Genesis to Revelation will provide you a refreshing look at God's word.

You are invited to embrace the scriptures and write your own affirmations and prayers. I hope you share the scriptures with family and friends. I know that my family and friends are glad that I did

January

January 1

GROWING IN THE FAITH

For this very reason, make every effort to add to your faith goodness; and to goodness, knowledge; and to knowledge, self-control; and to self-control, perseverance; and to perseverance, godliness; and to godliness, mutual affection; and to mutual affection, love.
—2 Peter 1:5–7 (NIV)

Affirmation/Prayer: I will never achieve perfection when it comes to trusting and serving God. Each day I will add a little to my faith to help me grow mentally, emotionally, and spiritually. Effort, not perfection, is the key to my being faithful. Thank you, Lord, for your spirit that gives me love, knowledge, self-control, hope, courage, and perseverance. Help me to continue to grow in the faith.

God is my source!

January 2

FEELINGS

I have told you these things, so that in me you may have peace. In this world you will have trouble. But take heart! I have overcome the world.
—John 16:33 (NIV)

Affirmation/Prayer: To think I will live a life free from trouble is living in an unrealistic world. When trouble comes, feelings of fear, sadness, loneliness, hurt, or anger may overtake me if I give in to these feelings. Thank you, Jesus, that in you, I have another choice. I can experience feelings of courage, strength, love, joy, and peace in spite of my troubles. Now I will let "He who is in you is greater than he who is in the world" 1 John 4:4 (NKJV)" be the ultimate guide to how I think or feel.

God is my source!

January 3

FIGHT OR FLIGHT

But understand this, that in the last days there will come times of difficulty. For people will be lovers of self, lovers of money, proud, arrogant, abusive, disobedient to their parents, ungrateful, unholy, heartless, unappeasable, slanderous, without self-control, brutal, not loving good, treacherous, reckless, swollen with conceit, lovers of pleasure rather than lovers of God, having the appearance of godliness, but denying its power. Avoid such people.
—2 Timothy 3:1–5 (ESV)

Put everything to the test. Accept what is good and don't have anything to do with evil.
—1 Thessalonians 5:21–22 (CEV)

Affirmation/Prayer: Lord, may I always be aware of my own weaknesses. Help me to set healthy boundaries avoid people and places that are not good for me or my walk with you. In doing so may I remember to love everyone as you have loved me.

God is my source!

January 4

HOPE, PATIENCE, AND PRAYER

Let your hope make you glad. Be patient in time of trouble and never stop praying.
—Romans 12:12 (CEV)

Affirmation/prayer: All I need to succeed today are hope, patience, and prayer. Hope fills my heart with expectations and trust in God. Patience helps me wait on God and tolerate others as well as tolerate unexpected delays. Prayer helps me relax and give everything to God. I will let hope, patience, and prayer dictate how I deal with people and circumstances outside of myself.

God is my source!

January 5

ANXIETY

When anxiety was great within me, your consolation brought me joy.
—Psalms 94:19 (NIV)

Do not be anxious about anything, but in every situation, by prayer and petition, with thanksgiving, present your requests to God. And the peace of God, which transcends all understanding, will guard your hearts and your minds in Christ Jesus.
—Philippians 4:6–7 (NIV)

Affirmation/prayer: Anxiety is great within me when I try to predict what will happen in the future. The worry and restlessness I feel are the results of my always anticipating the worst-case scenario. This is the result of my wanting to be in control. Lord, instead of holding on to thoughts that only lead to fear and doubt, I will put my future in your hands through prayer and meditation.

Thank you for your gift of peace that passes all understanding.

God is my source!

January 6

THE LIGHT

Jesus told us God is light and doesn't have any darkness in him. Now we are telling you. If we claim to have fellowship with him and yet walk in the darkness, we lie and do not live out the truth. But if we are living in the light, as God is in the light, then we have fellowship with each other, and the blood of Jesus, his Son, cleanses us from all sin.
—1 John 1:5–7 (NIV)

Affirmation/prayer: To walk in darkness or the light of God is my choice. When I walk in the heavenly light, God is my companion and my guide. God is the light that guides me away from darkness. Following the light helps me see the lies that I tell myself when it comes to my relationship with God, myself, and others. As I walk closer to God, the darkness of my past is left behind. In his light I feel warmth, joy, serenity, and peace. Thanking Jesus for his grace that allows me to walk in the light.

God is my source!

January 7

FOLLOWING GOOD ADVICE

How happy is the man who does not follow the advice of the wicked or take the path of sinners or join a group of mockers! Instead, his delight is in the LORD's instruction, and he meditates on it day and night. He is like a tree planted beside streams of water that bears its fruit in season and whose leaf does not wither. Whatever he does prospers.
—Psalms 1:1–3 (HCSB)

Affirmation/prayer: There are times and situations when the right path to take may not be so obvious. Thank you, God, for your words of wisdom that teach me how to live. When I am in doubt, Lord, give me the patience to pray and meditate on your instructions. Strength and blessings come from listening to your instructions and doing the right thing. May I be like the tree that is planted by the water whose leaf does not wither.

God is my source!

January 8

DECISIONS, DECISIONS, DECISIONS

See then that ye walk circumspectly, not as fools, but as wise, Redeeming the time, because the days are evil. Wherefore be ye not unwise, but understanding what the will of the Lord is.
—Ephesians 5:15–17 (NKJV)

Affirmation/prayer: I know that when it comes to making decisions (important or not), God knows what needs to be done. Lord, please help me not act as a fool when making decisions, especially those that must be made without delay. When time is needed to think things through, I ask for patience and your wisdom from above to do your will.

God is my source!

January 9

DEPRESSION

As the deer pants for streams of water, so my soul pants for you, my God.

My tears have been my meat day and night, while they continually say unto me, where is thy God?

Why, my soul, are you downcast? Why so disturbed within me? Put your hope in God, for I will yet praise him, my Savior and my God.
—Psalms 42:1, 3, 5 (ESV)

Affirmation/prayer: There are times when I am down. The magic eraser for these times is hope in the living God. Depression is lifted when I am not focused on the problem but on the God I serve. He has blessed, is blessing, and will continue to bless me all of my life. God is my source! I will put my faith in him.

God is my source!

January 10

REJECTION: I AM LOVABLE

The LORD appeared to us in the past, saying: "I have loved you with an everlasting love."
—Jeremiah 31:3 (NIV)

We love because he first loved us.
—1 John 4:19 (NIV)

Affirmation/prayer: Lord, your words tells me that I am loved by you. Sometimes I feel alone and unloved by anyone. When this world rejects me and I don't seem to love myself, remind me that I am loved by you. Your love is everlasting, not the conditional love that this world has to offer. Help me love myself as you love me unconditionally. I am never unloved because you, Lord, You are my source of unconditional love.

God is my source!

January 11

GROWING PAINS

Not only so, but we also glory in our sufferings, because we know that suffering produces perseverance; perseverance, character; and character, hope. And hope does not put us to shame, because God's love has been poured out into our hearts through the Holy Spirit, who has been given to us.
—Romans 5:3–5 (NIV)

Affirmation/prayer: If it were not for the things that I have suffered through in this life, I would not have grown to be the strong person I am today. Suffering through lean times teaches the importance of being thankful in the good times. Suffering through someone walking out taught me that I am stronger that I think. It also taught me the meaning of love and to choose wisely those I would love. Facing my fears taught me that I don't have to fear the unknown. Pain in my body has taught me to take care of the body God gave me. Suffering through the criticism of others taught me that it is not what others say about me but what I say about myself that counts. All of these things taught me to put my trust in Jesus. In him there is a living hope, healing, growth, and my salvation.

God is my source!

January 12

MY NEEDS

And this is the confidence that we have in him, that, if we ask any thing according to his will, he heareth us: And if we know that he hears us, whatsoever we ask, we know that we have the petitions that we desired of him.
—1 John 5:14–15 (KJV)

Affirmation/prayer: Thank you, Lord, for hearing my prayers about the things I need. As I pray according to your will and not my greed, I can always have the confidence that You will meet all my needs.

God is my source!

January 13

GROWTH

Good people will prosper like palm trees, and they will grow strong like the cedars of Lebanon. They will take root in your house, LORD God, and they will do well. They will still bear fruit in old age, they will stay fresh and green.
—Psalms 92:12–14 (CEV)

Let your roots grow down into him, and let your lives be built on him. Then your faith will grow strong in the truth you were taught, and you will overflow with thankfulness.
—Colossians 2:7 (NLT)

Affirmation/prayer: My faith in God is like deep roots anchored in good soil. It nourishes and quenches the thirst of the soul. When I am feeling tired, empty and alone, I will anchor myself in God and his word. Just as the roots of a tree are the anchors that keep the tree standing during a storm, my strength comes from my faith in God and his word. The fruit of this relationship is knowledge, greater faith, service, and a thankful heart. The more I am rooted in God, the more I will serve him and others. Lord, help me stay close to you so that I may remain fruitful all of the days of my life.

God is my source!

January 14

THY WILL BE DONE

Pray like this: Our Father in heaven, may your name be kept holy. May your Kingdom come soon. May your will be done on earth, as it is in heaven.
—Matthew 6:9–10 (NLT)

Now honor the LORD, the God of your ancestors, and do his will...
—Ezra 10:11 (NIV)

Affirmation/prayer: Lord, may I be accepting of your will for me. May I recognize that the things that are not part of my life may not be your will for me. May I also recognize that the things that are to be part of my life will come. Thy will be done.

God is my source!

January 15

A NEW WAY OF THINKING

Finally, brothers and sisters, whatever is true, whatever is noble, whatever is right, whatever is pure, whatever is lovely, whatever is admirable—if anything is excellent or praiseworthy—think about such things.
—Philippians 4:8 (NIV)

Affirmation/prayer: What happens to me in life is less important than the way I perceive the situation. I can condition my mind to think on the positive, not the negative; more hope, not defeat; more joy, not sadness; more peace, not confusion. I may not be able change the situation or people, but I can train my mind with prayer and meditation to think on the positive side of life. The giants in my life become smaller and more manageable when I see them as just one more thing that me and my God can handle.

God is my source!

January 16

LIFE WORTH LIVING

Do not love the world or anything in the world. If anyone loves the world, love for the Father is not in them. For everything in the world—the lust of the flesh, the lust of the eyes, and the pride of life—comes not from the Father but from the world. The world and its desires pass away, but whoever does the will of God lives forever.
—1 John 2:15–17 (NIV)

Affirmation/prayer: When I love the things of this world more than God, I lose my way. Pride keeps me constantly comparing myself to others as better than others or less than. Wanting everything I see has me chasing after more stuff. Constantly satisfying my cravings binds me to habitual things not good for my mind, body, or soul. Lord, help me focus on loving you more than this world. I give you complete control. In you I can live a life worth living.

God is my source!

January 17

DON'T RUN

The wicked run away when no one is chasing them, but the godly are as bold as lions.
—Proverbs 28:1 (NLT)

Therefore put on the full armor of God, so that when the day of evil comes, you may be able to stand your ground, and after you have done everything, to stand.
—Ephesians 6:13 (NIV)

Affirmation/prayer: Life has taught me that problems will not just disappear because I refused to face them. Instead of running away from problems, I ask the Holy Spirit to help me use the spiritual power and knowledge within to solve them. When I have done all within my power, I will turn to God, who is able to save me.

When in doubt I will not run but stand my ground and give it to God, who already knows what I am to do.

God is my source!

January 18

TEMPTATIONS

No temptation has overtaken you except what is common to mankind. And God is faithful; he will not let you be tempted beyond what you can bear. But when you are tempted, he will also provide a way out so that you can endure it.
—1 Corinthians 10:13 (NIV)

Affirmation/prayer: God is faithful and is able to help me stand against each and every temptation that comes my way. I will take an honest inventory of my weaknesses and temptations and give them to God. Lord, I ask for the faith and courage to walk away from any temptation that would defeat me and separates me from you.

God is my source!

January 19

FREEDOM

So if the Son sets you free, you will be free indeed.
—John 8:36 (NIV)

Now the Lord is the Spirit, and where the Spirit of the Lord is, there is freedom.
—2 Corinthians 3:17 (NIV)

Affirmation/prayer: To me, freedom means that I need not be a slave to the ideas and opinion of others. I am free to be the person that God has created me to be. Jesus has given me his spirit, which frees me from the things of this world. Habits no longer control the way I think or act. He is my living hope. In Him I have found what freedom really means.

God is my source!

January 20

NO CONDEMNATION

There is therefore now no condemnation to them which are in Christ Jesus, who walk not after the flesh, but after the Spirit.
—Romans 8:1 (KJV)

Do not judge, and you will not be judged. Do not condemn, and you will not be condemned. Forgive, and you will be forgiven.
—Luke 6:37 (NIV)

Affirmation/prayer: I will not judge my actions harshly because this causes me to live in shame or guilt. Nor will I condemn others. I will leave the judging to God. He alone truly knows a man's heart. Holy Spirit, guide me and lead me in the way of forgiveness because there is no condemnation for those who are in Christ. It is by forgiving, not judging, that others are led to Christ. Help me to forgive myself and others as you forgive me when mistakes are made.

God is my source!

January 21

NEVER STOP PRAYING

Finally, I confessed all my sins to you and stopped trying to hide my guilt. I said to myself, "I will confess my rebellion to the LORD." And you forgave me! All my guilt is gone. Therefore, let all the godly pray to you while there is still time, For you are my hiding place; you protect me from trouble…The LORD says, "I will guide you along the best pathway for your life. I will advise you and watch over you.
—Psalms 32:5–8 (NLT)

Never stop praying.
—1 Thessalonians 5:17 (NLT)

Affirmation/prayer: I will never stop praying, and God will never stop listening. As I am his child, God desires to hear my prayers, and he will keep me in times of trouble. I will not wait until life becomes too much before, I talk to God. When I pray guilt and shame disappear. The more I pray, the wiser and stronger I am in him. He always has his eye on me therefore, all I need is to keep my eyes on him. Thank you, God, for listening to my prayers. Even on my best days, I still need to talk to you.

God is my source!

January 22

I FALL DOWN

The LORD told me to say to his people, "When someone falls down, doesn't he get back up? If someone misses the road, doesn't he turn back?
—Jeremiah 8:4 (GNT)

The LORD helps the fallen and lifts those bent beneath their loads.
—Psalms 145:14 (NLT)

Affirmation/prayer: When I fall in life, and sometime I will fall, I will not be afraid to try again with God on my side. Jesus, my Lord, please lead me in the right direction so that I may not get lost or stumble. Remove regret and procrastination, and replace them with the courage to keep moving forward, knowing that you are on my side. Thank you, Lord, that when I fall, you are always there to lift me up. Jesus, you are my source; lift me up and show me the right way to go.

God is my source!

January 23

ASK, SEEK, FIND

When one door of happiness closes, another opens; but often we look so long at the closed door that we do not see the one which has been opened for us.
—Helen Keller

Ask and it will be given to you; seek and you will find; knock and the door will be opened to you. For everyone who asks receives; the one who seeks finds; and to the one who knocks, the door will be opened.
—Matthew 7:7–8 (NIV)

Affirmation/prayer: God is waiting for me to seek his help with my goals and aspirations.

God is waiting for me to seek his help with the things that trouble me.

God is waiting for me to relax and hear his voice.

God is always waiting to open doors for me. I only need to ask him and seek his will.

Lord, open my eyes so that I will not focus on the closed doors. Show me how to ask, seek, and find opportunities that are waiting for me.

God is my source!

January 24

ALL THINGS

I can do all things through him who strengthens me.
—Philippians 4:13 (ISV)

Affirmation/prayer: This verse reminds me that God often works through me by giving me the strength to do the things I need to do. "I can do" means I have a part to play in God's strengthening me. Lord, please erase all negative thinking from my mind. Lord, give me the courage to do all the things you would have me to do. With you there are no impossibilities.

God is my source!

January 25

POSITIVELY SPEAKING

A good man brings good things out of the good stored up in his heart, and an evil man brings evil things out of the evil stored up in his heart. For the mouth speaks what the heart is full of.
—Luke 6:45 (NIV)

Affirmation/prayer: Lord, remove hatred, bitterness, envy, and pride from my heart so that I may speak positive words to others. Fill my heart with the love, forgiveness, joy, and peace so that the words I speak to others will reflect the love you have for all. Fill my heart with a good self-image so that my self-talk will be loving and positive. Fill my heart with thanksgiving so that I may forever praise your name.

Positively speaking Lord, you are awesome.

God is my source!

January 26

REENERGIZED

Then, because so many people were coming and going that they did not even have a chance to eat, he said to them, "Come with me by yourselves to a quiet place and get some rest." So they went away by themselves in a boat to a solitary place.
—Mark 6:31–32 (NIV)

Affirmation/prayer: In life sometimes, I need to let go of the daily "busyness" to focus on spiritual and inner healing. Jesus is my perfect example of the need for quiet time and solitude. Prayer gives me an opportunity to listen to God as he teaches me how to deal with any unhealthy thoughts. I am reenergized in this quiet time as I feel God's healing power of hope, love, and peace. Lord, reenergize me in my quiet times of prayer.

God is my source!

January 27

BLESS THE LORD

Bless the LORD, O my soul, and forget not all his benefits.
—Psalms 103:2 (ESV)

Not that I am speaking of being in need, for I have learned in whatever situation I am to be content. I know how to be brought low, and I know how to abound. In any and every circumstance, I have learned the secret of facing plenty and hunger, abundance and need.
—Philippians 4:11–12 (ESV)

Affirmation/prayer: Your word teaches me that the secret of living a life of contentment and peace is to thank You daily for your blessings. My contentment is not in things. It is in how I choose to view my life. When I constantly complain about things, I am only living in negativity. Therefore, I will make a habit of praising God, even for the little things that go well. I will praise God in times of plenty, for I am blessed. In times of lack, I am still blessed because I know that God provides. I have seen that better days always come. Thank you, Lord, for all that I have.

God is my source!

January 28

DISCIPLINE

Do you not know that in a race all the runners run, but only one gets the prize? Run in such a way as to get the prize. Everyone who competes in the games goes into strict training. They do it to get a crown that will not last, but we do it to get a crown that will last forever. Therefore, I do not run like someone running aimlessly; I do not fight like a boxer beating the air. No, I strike a blow to my body and make it my slave so that after I have preached to others, I myself will not be disqualified for the prize.
—1 Corinthians 9:24–27 (NIV)

Affirmation/prayer: Jesus, please help me, through prayer and meditation and following your word. Train my mind, body, and spirit so that I will obtain a more disciplined life. You know me; therefore, I pray for wisdom to set realistic, obtainable goals for my life. I pray that I will not give up when things go wrong. My problems will become my strength and character builders when I follow your lead. Lord, help me not run any race aimlessly, especially the race to one day be with you in heaven.

God is my source!

January 29

MAKING LIFE EASIER

Take my yoke upon you and learn from me, for I am gentle and humble in heart, and you will find rest for your souls. For my yoke is easy and my burden is light.
—Matthew 11:29–30 (NIV)

Affirmation/prayer: Your word tells me that life does not have to be so difficult. I will stop trying to force life to happen in my own way and in my own time. You are willing and able, Lord, to take my stresses and cares of this world. I find peace in my soul as I take all my burdens off my shoulders and give them to you.

God is my source!

January 30

BLESSINGS

May the LORD bless you and protect you. May the LORD smile on you and be gracious to you. May the LORD show you his favor and give you his peace.
—Numbers 6:24–26 (NLT)

Amen!

Affirmation/prayer: Thank you for your blessings, Lord. They give me joy.

God is my source!

January 31

I AM GOD'S CREATION

I praise you because I am fearfully and wonderfully made; your works are wonderful; I know that full well.
—Psalms 139:14 (NIV)

"For I know the plans I have for you," declares the LORD, "plans to prosper you and not to harm you, plans to give you hope and a future."
—Jeremiah 29:11 (NIV)

Affirmation/prayer: Jesus, help me to embrace and love your handiwork: me. Lord, forgive me when I criticize myself after making a mistake for when I misjudge situations, I am only being human. Lord, point out the wonderful gifts that you have given me. Lead me forward into the future that your hands have planned for me. I eagerly await seeing all you have in store for me. Thank you for the love that was shown when you created me!

God is my source!

February

February 1

OLD HABITS DIE HARD

What shall we say, then? Shall we go on sinning so that grace may increase? Of course not! Since we have died to sin, how can we continue to live in it?

We know that our old sinful selves were crucified with Christ so that sin might lose its power in our lives. We are no longer slaves to sin.

For when we died with Christ, we were set free from the power of sin.

Do not let sin control the way you live; do not give in to sinful desires.

—Romans 6:1–2, 6–7, 12 (NLV)

Affirmation/prayer: Some say that "old habits die hard." Sometimes I say, "I have prayed for Jesus to forgive me, but I just can't stop this bad habit". The truth is Jesus did not give me his forgiveness and grace so that I can be a slave to myself. Knowing the love he has for me, I no longer say, "I can't" but pray for wisdom, and love to remove any bad habits that are destroying my mind, body, and soul. Old habits die as his power gives me the strength to live a better life.

God is my source!

February 2

PEACE OF MIND

Do not be anxious about anything, but in every situation, by prayer and petition, with thanksgiving, present your requests to God. And the peace of God, which transcends all understanding, will guard your hearts and your minds in Christ Jesus.
—Philippians 4:6–7 (NIV)

Affirmation/prayer: I give everything to God and accept his peace "which passeth all understanding." Jesus, guard my heart and keep me from loving people and things that will only hurt me in the long run. I pray that you will remove worry, doubt, and any anxious thoughts and replace them with peace of mind. When things happen and I don't know why, I pray for peace. Thank you for your many blessings. It is because of your love, that I have peace that is above all understanding. Thank you Jesus for peace of mind.

God is my source!

February 3

A MARVELOUS CREATION

I praise you because I am fearfully and wonderfully made; your works are wonderful; I know that full well.
—Psalms 139:14 (NIV)

Affirmation/prayer: I will love myself just as God has created me. I will be true to my thoughts, feelings, hopes, and dreams. My soul knows who I am, so I will get in touch with the beautiful person inside. I won't try to be anyone else. I will live my life and show the world this beautiful work of art that God has created. I praise God for his marvelous creation: me.

God is my source!

February 4

USE ME, LORD

So let's not get tired of doing what is good. At just the right time we will reap a harvest of blessing if we don't give up. Therefore, whenever we have the opportunity, we should do good to everyone...
—Galatians 6:9–10 (NLT)

May the Lord deal kindly with you...
—Ruth 1:8 (NIV)

Affirmation/prayer: Jesus, use me in the mainstream of life. Please let me live a life that is rewarding to other people. Let me not get tired even when family and friends seem ungrateful. Help me remember that as long as I am doing your will, you will repay in more ways than I can imagine. Most of all, thank you Lord for being kind to me. I am blessed as you use me to serve others.

God is my source!

February 5

DON'T GIVE UP

My flesh and my heart may fail, but God is the strength of my heart and my portion forever.
—Psalms 73:26 (NIV)

That is why we never give up. Though our bodies are dying, our spirits are being renewed every day.

-

So we don't look at the troubles we can see now; rather, we fix our gaze on things that cannot be seen. For the things we see now will soon be gone, but the things we cannot see will last forever.
—2 Corinthians 4:16, 18 (NLT)

Affirmation/prayer: Lord, you are my eternal strength, hope, and the answer for all my problems today and the life to come. I won't give up.

God is my source!

February 6

REMEMBERING

But God demonstrates his own love for us in this: While we were still sinners, Christ died for us.
—Romans 5:8 (NIV)

Affirmation/prayer: Remembering what God did for me because of his love brightens my spirit. Sharing what God has done with someone else brings that joy back to me.

I will share my story. I will share Christ and the gospel message. I will share his love.

God is my source!

February 7

HE'S WAITING

Cast all your anxiety on him because he cares for you.
—1 Peter 5:7 (NIV)

Affirmation/prayer: God wants me to depend on him more than any other relationship. Each day he is waiting with outstretched hands to help and guide me. Each day he is waiting to give me peace.

God is my source!

February 8

GOD, MY EVERYTHING

Whom do I have in heaven but You? And I desire nothing on earth but You. My flesh and my heart may fail but God is the strength of my heart my portion forever.
—Psalms 73:25–26

May He give you what your heart desires and fulfill your whole purpose.
—Psalms 20:4 (HCSB)

Affirmation/prayer: Nothing that this world has to offer me has satisfied me like God. Instead of looking to others to be the main source of well-being, I will turn to God. God is my source. God is my strength. God is all that I need. God is my everything.

God is my source!

February 9

BE ENCOURAGED

The heavens declare the glory of God; the skies proclaim the work of his hands. Day after day they pour forth speech; night after night they reveal knowledge. They have no speech, they use no words; no sound is heard from them. Yet their voice goes out into all the earth, their words to the ends of the world. In the heavens God has pitched a tent for the sun.
—Psalms 19:1–4 (NIV)

Affirmation/prayer: When I gaze into the sky, day or night, I can see the awesomeness of God. I can hear nature whisper to me, "God has not left you; he is right here." May I remember that above the clouds of life, the stars are still twinkling, and the sun still shines. Be encouraged!

God is my source!

February 10

GOD LOVES ME

"Though the mountains be shaken and the hills be removed, yet my unfailing love for you will not be shaken nor my covenant of peace be removed," says the LORD, who has compassion on you.
—Isaiah 54:10 (NIV)

For God so loved the world, that he gave his only begotten Son, that whosoever believes in him should not perish, but have everlasting life.
—John 3:16 (NKJV)

Affirmation/prayer: God loves me. No ifs, no buts, no maybes. God's love for me is unshakable. Some days it is difficult to remember this because in this world people will love you today and forget you tomorrow. It is not God's love for me that is the question but my love for him. Thank you, God, for your unshakable love.

God is my source!

February 11

SEARCH ME, TEST ME, LEAD ME

Search me, God, and know my heart; test me and know my anxious thoughts. Point out anything in me that offends you, and lead me along the path of everlasting life.
—Psalms 139:23–24 (NLT)

Now this is what the LORD of the Heavenly Armies, says: "Carefully consider your ways…"
—Haggai 1:5 (ISV)

Affirmation/prayer: I know there are some bad habits that I have and prefer to pretend they don't exist. I pray, Lord, that you search my heart and make me aware of my destructive and sometimes sinful behaviors. Give me the strength to conquer any spiritual, physical, or emotional bad habits that lead to my destruction.

Test my thoughts of fear, envy, pride, ego, and self-reliance. Gently lead me, I pray, to a better way of living that blesses me and honors your name.

God is my source!

February 12

STINKY THINKING

We demolish arguments and every pretension that sets itself up against the knowledge of God, and we take captive every thought to make it obedient to Christ.
—2 Corinthians 10:5 (NIV)

Affirmation/prayer: Today, I am a failure.

1. I am not good enough.
2. God does not love me.
3. I can't shake this habit.
4. Everyone gets blessed but me.

These stinky thoughts that cripple me are not from God. Lord, help me take hold of all negative and sinful thinking and give it to you. Lord, remind me daily of who I am as your child. Through your words I replace can replace stinky thinking with positive affirmations.

1. I can do all things through Christ.
2. I am beautiful and wonderfully made.
3. I am loved and blessed by God.
4. He will never leave me or forsake me.

God is my source!

February 13

BEING ME

For in him we live and move and have our being. As some of your own poets have said, "We are his offspring."
—Acts 17:28 (NIV)

Affirmation/prayer: Everything I have been, everything I am, and everything I will be is because of God. When I look at life from that perspective, it takes off the pressure of living. Thank you, Lord, for everything. Thank you, Jesus, that I can be called your child. *You* give me the power to live, to move, and to be who I am (*me*). Knowing who I am gives me strength and peace.

God is my source!

February 14

CRUTCHES

Someone will say, "I am allowed to do anything." Yes; but not everything is good for you. I could say that I am allowed to do anything, but I am not going to let anything make me its slave.
—1 Corinthians 6:12 (GNT)

Affirmation/prayer: I gotta have it! That is the phrase that keeps me enslaved. God, release me of anyone or anything that was once a healthy support system but is now my crutch. Release the fear of letting go of crutches so that I may give them to you, Lord. Give me the strength and courage to live a better life. May I remember:

God is my source!

February 15

I WILL BE OKAY

We are hard pressed on every side, but not crushed; perplexed, but not in despair; persecuted, but not abandoned; struck down, but not destroyed.

All this is for your benefit, so that the grace that is reaching more and more people may cause thanksgiving to overflow to the glory of God.

Therefore we do not lose heart. Though outwardly we are wasting away, yet inwardly we are being renewed day by day.

—2 Corinthians 4:8–9, 15–16 (NIV)

Affirmation/prayer: I used to ask why I must suffer sickness, divorce, death, deception by friends, lack of finances, and so forth. I now know that in this world, no one is free from its pain and suffering. I have found out that when I give my suffering to you, Lord, I am strengthened, not destroyed, by them.

God, as you strengthen me, may my trials be a witness to others of your strength, power, goodness, and grace.

I will be okay.

God is my source!

February 16

KNOWLEDGE VERSUS FAITH

I don't really understand myself, for I want to do what is right, but I don't do it. Instead, I do what I hate. But if I know that what I am doing is wrong, this shows that I agree that the law is good.

I want to do what is good, but I don't. I don't want to do what is wrong, but I do it anyway.

What a wretched man I am! Who will rescue me from this body that is subject to death?
—Romans 7:15–16, 19, 24 (NLT)

Affirmation/prayer: Knowledge of God's word in my head is not enough. I realize that only faith in God can deliver me from death resulting from my destructive behaviors. I need faith in God. Jesus delivers today from the things that I do in mind body, spirit, and soul that are destroying me.

Not my will but thy will be done.

God is my source!

February 17

FOOD FOR LIFE

He humbled you and let you be hungry, and fed you with manna which you did not know, nor did your fathers know, that He might make you understand that man does not live by bread alone, but man lives by everything that proceeds out of the mouth of the LORD.
—Deuteronomy 8:3 (ESV)

But he answered, "It is written, 'Man shall not live by bread alone, but by every word that comes from the mouth of God.'"
—Matthew 4:4 (EST)

Affirmation/prayer: The word of God is food for my soul. Just as my physical body requires nutrients, it also needs spiritual food. May I not fall into the trap of thinking that material things alone can give me happiness. I submit to your will. I humbly ask that you feed my body, spirit, and soul. In you alone I am complete.

God is my source!

February 18

DREAM BIG

For all the animals of the forest are mine, and I own the cattle on a thousand hills. I know every bird in the mountains, and the insects in the fields are mine. If I were hungry, I would not tell you, for all the world is mine and everything in it.
—Psalms 50:10–12 (NLT)

Affirmation/prayer: When I include God, I can view the world outside of my limited circle of life. With God my view of life and its possibilities are limitless. People and things that I once feared and thought to be so very important in life have become insignificant, and life is less fearful.

Lord, you are my source! You, Lord, own and control this world. I will move above and beyond my limited thinking and abilities and put my future into your hands.

Help me, Lord, to dream big.

God is my source!

February 19

PEACEFUL MINDFULNESS

You will keep in perfect peace all who trust in you, all whose thoughts are fixed on you! Trust in the LORD always, for the LORD God is the eternal Rock.
—Isaiah 26:3–4 (NLT)

Affirmation/prayer: If I can keep from thinking of things that can or might go wrong and keep my eyes on God, this will be a peaceful day. God, you are my strength for today. I may not be able to change my circumstances, but I can be sure that God will give me the peace I need to deal with it. May I be mindful of your presence. Lord, help me be at peace by trusting and focusing on you. Thank you, Lord, for your peace.

God is my source!

February 20

IT'S JUST NOT FAIR

Do not fret because of those who are evil or be envious of those who do wrong; for like the grass they will soon wither, like green plants they will soon die away. Trust in the LORD and do good. Then you will live safely in the land and prosper. Take delight in the LORD, and he will give you the desires of your heart.

Be still before the LORD and wait patiently for him; do not fret when people succeed in their ways, when they carry out their wicked schemes. Refrain from anger and turn from wrath; do not fret—it leads only to evil.
—Psalms 37:1–4, 7–8 (NIV)

Affirmation/prayer: It's just not fair! May I not have a pity party knowing that you, Lord, are just in all your ways. Help me set healthy boundaries when dealing with those who do not have my best interest at heart. God, please remove all hidden anger, envy, and jealousy of others from my heart. Lord, give me wisdom and patience when dealing with unfair people. Remind me that you will deal with wrongdoers in your time, not mine. Show me the path I should take to receive my blessings.

God is my source!

February 21

HE'S WAITING

Cast all your anxiety on him because he cares for you.
—1 Peter 5:7 (NIV)

Affirmation/prayer: God wants me to depend on him more than any other relationship. Each day he is waiting with outstretched hands to help and guide me.

God is my source!

February 22

THE WAY

My sheep listen to my voice; I know them, and they follow me.
—John 10:27 (NIV)

Whether you turn to the right or to the left, your ears will hear a voice behind you, saying, "This is the way; walk in it."
—Isaiah 30:21 (NIV)

Affirmation/prayer: I won't get lost in the hustle and bustle of today if I just take a moment to hear God's voice. Thank God he knows what lies ahead. I know the way when I follow your voice.

God is my source!

February 23

A NEW DAY

Because of the LORD's great love we are not consumed, for his compassions never fail. They are new every morning; great is your faithfulness. I say to myself, "The LORD is my portion; therefore, I will wait for him." The LORD is good to those whose hope is in him, to the one who seeks him; it is good to wait quietly for the salvation of the LORD.
—Lamentations 3:22–26 (NIV)

Affirmation/prayer: Every morning God has just what I need to face another day. Every morning God has new blessings just waiting for me to receive them. Every morning I can count on God to be faithful. Every morning I can expect to receive God's compassion, mercy, and grace. Every day I will wait on God to receive his blessings. Every day as I face problems, I will seek God and put my hope and faith in the Lord. Thank you, Lord, for your faithful promises that never ends. Thank you, Lord.

God is my source!

February 24

FEAR

My heart pounds in my chest. The terror of death assaults me. Fear and trembling overwhelm me, and I can't stop shaking. Oh, that I had wings like a dove; then I would fly away and rest!

Give your burdens to the LORD, and he will take care of you. He will not permit the godly to slip and fall.
—Psalms 55:4–6, 22 (NLT)

Affirmation/prayer: I know in this world I am only human. Daily I am reminded of the things that can destroy me. I am not troubled when I trust God to take care of me. Fear is replaced by calmness and peace. Like a dove flies away from danger, I find peace and protection of the Father through prayer.

God is my source!

February 25

MADE IN HIS IMAGE

Then God said, "Let us make human beings in our image, to be like us...
—Genesis 1:26 (NLT)

Affirmation/prayer: There is something to be said about God having made me in his image. I pray, Lord, for your guidance to live out a life that reflects your divine purpose. When I question who I am, remind me that you made me and have all the answers for my purpose in this life. Lord, thanks to your design, I can live a life that reflects you—a life that is filled with purpose and love.

God is my source!

February 26

THE SPIRIT

The wind blows wherever it pleases. You hear its sound, but you cannot tell where it comes from or where it is going. So it is with everyone born of the Spirit.
—John 3:8 (NIV)

Peter replied, "Repent and be baptized, every one of you, in the name of Jesus Christ for the forgiveness of your sins. And you will receive the gift of the Holy Spirit.
—Acts 2:38 (NIV)

Affirmation/prayer: I don't understand how God fills me with his Spirit. I am just glad he does. In it I have love, joy, peace, forbearance, kindness, goodness, faithfulness, gentleness, and self-control.

God is my source!

February 27

UNEXPECTED BLESSINGS

*And all these blessings shall come upon you and overtake you, if
you obey the voice of the LORD your God. You will be blessed in
the city and blessed in the country.*
—Deuteronomy 28:2–3 (NIV)

Affirmation/prayer: I know that life is much easier when I
do things God's way. Unexpected blessings have come my way
and overtaken me because of the goodness of others. May I be
an unexpected blessing in someone's life today.

God is my source!

February 28

ESCAPING TEMPTATIONS

The temptations in your life are no different from what others experience. And God is faithful. He will not allow the temptation to be more than you can stand. When you are tempted, he will show you a way out so that you can endure.
—1 Corinthians 10:13 (NLT)

We destroy every proud obstacle that keeps people from knowing God. We capture their rebellious thoughts and teach them to obey Christ.
—2 Corinthians 10:5 (NLT)

Affirmation/prayer: It may look good or feel good, but is it in my best interest? Satan knows my weaknesses. There will always be things in life that tempt me to satisfy my flesh, despite the devastating consequences of my actions. There will always be people in this world who do not have my best interests at heart. Today I know that God has already provided an escape plan for any and every temptation. As I read your words, Lord, help me change my thoughts and make my way of escape clear.

God is my source!

February 29

MY HEART

Above all else, guard your heart, for everything you do flows from it.
—Proverbs 4:23 (NIV)

I will give you a new heart and put a new spirit in you; I will remove from you your heart of stone and give you a heart of flesh.
—Ezekiel 36:26 (NIV)

God, create a pure heart in me, and renew a right attitude within me.
—Psalms 51:10 (ISV)

Affirmation/prayer: I will look inside to examine and strengthen my spiritual beliefs. For the beliefs I hold dear are the guiding factors of how I respond to life. God, look into my heart and show me the negative beliefs that defeat me. Fill my heart with the belief that through you, all things are possible. Fill my heart with hope for a better, brighter future.

God is my source!

March

March 1

YOUR LOVE

Your love, LORD, reaches to the heavens, your faithfulness to the skies. Your righteousness is like the highest mountains, your justice like the great deep…How priceless is your unfailing love, O God! People take refuge in the shadow of your wings.
—Psalms 36:5–7 (NIV)

The LORD is good, a refuge in times of trouble. He cares for those who trust in him.
—Nahum 1:7 (NIV)

Affirmation/prayer: The love that you have for me, Lord, is above my comprehension. I can't put it into the box of my human reasoning because it just does not fit. No money on earth can buy your love, yet you give it to me without cost. No power on earth can break it, yet you use it to give me strength. No matter where I go, your love is there to protect me. Your love says to me, "Trust me in difficult times, for I will give you protection and peace." Praise God for the love he has given me.

God is my source!

March 2

PERFECT LOVE

There is no fear in love. But perfect love drives out fear, because fear has to do with punishment. The one who fears is not made perfect in love. We love because he first loved us.
—1 John 4:18–19 (NIV)

Affirmation/prayer: Thank you, Lord, for loving me and giving me the Spirit of love. I don't have to be afraid of your love because it is perfect. Knowing that there are no flaws in your love shows me how I should love other people. God, give me the wisdom and power to cast out the fear of punishment when it comes to loving you. Teach me how to love others. Show me how to love those things that are truly beautiful inside me and others.

God is my source!

March 3

THE WORD

Remember your promise to me; it is my only hope.
—Psalms 119:49 (NLT)

Affirmation/prayer: Lord, thank you for your word. It reminds me of your grace. Grace that saved me once is still there and will be with me, not because of what I do or fail to do but because I am loved.

God is my source!

March 4

GOD'S WISDOM

For the foolishness of God is wiser than human wisdom, and the weakness of God is stronger than human strength.
—1 Corinthians 1:25 (NIV)

Affirmation/prayer: How foolish of me to think that I know better than you, Lord, when it comes to my life. How foolish of me to think I am strong enough to do everything on my own without your strength. How foolish of me to think the philosophies of man are wiser than your words of life. Now that I know better, I will do better. Jesus, give me wisdom and strength to live this day. Not only for today, Lord, but I pray that at the dawn of each and every day, you will do the same. Thank you for your blessing of wisdom and knowledge.

God is my source!

March 5

LETTING GOD BE FIRST

Don't worry and ask yourselves, "Will we have anything to eat? Will we have anything to drink? Will we have any clothes to wear?

But more than anything else, put God's work first and do what he wants. Then the other things will be yours as well.
—Matthew 6:31, 33 (CEV)

Affirmation/prayer: How much easier my day becomes when I put God first! My thoughts are less chaotic, and my way is clearer. When I love God more than money, work, or stuff, it is easier to do what he wants. Lord, please help me to put you above all.

God is my source!

March 6

SHAME

But the LORD God called to the man, "Where are you?" And he said, "I heard the sound of you in the garden, and I was afraid, because I was naked, and I hid myself."
—Genesis 3:9–10 (NIV)

For the Son of Man came to seek and save those who are lost.
—Luke 19:10 (NIV)

Affirmation/prayer: My shame drives me away from God. Repentance takes me to him. Just as God sought man in the garden when he was afraid and hid himself, Jesus is seeking to release me of my guilt and shame. Jesus loves me, and in Him there is no shame.

God is my source!

March 7

ALL THINGS

Before I was afflicted, I went astray, but now I obey your word.
—Psalms 119:67 (NIV)

And we know that God causes all things to work together for good to those who love God, to those who are called according to His purpose.
—Romans 8:28 (NIV)

Affirmation/prayer: Is it possible that my suffering, distress, pain, trouble, hardship, and adversity could be part of the all things working for my good? When I consider that it is God's purpose for my life and not my own purpose for living, the answer is yes. Lord, help to me see the lessons that come out of my trials. When I can see the good in all things, I can learn what I need to fulfill your purpose for my life. Lord, give to me your peace, your joy, your courage, and your strength as I go through all things in this life.

God is my source!

March 8

COMMITTED

Don't get tired of helping others. You will be rewarded when the time is right, if you don't give up.
—Galatians 6:9 (CEV)

Seek his will in all you do, and he will show you which path to take.
—Proverbs 3:6 (NLT)

Affirmation/prayer: God, show me your will in serving others. Before I commit to doing anything, help me know if this is in the best interests of those I would serve. Give me the courage to say no when asked to serve if it is not part of your plan. Remove fear when working in new places and meeting new people. Give me strength to keep the faith so that I will remain committed and not grow weary in doing good.

God is my source!

March 9

PRAYER AND STRENGTH

As soon as I pray, you answer me; you encourage me by giving me strength.
—Psalms 138:3 (NLT)

Look to the LORD AND HIS STRENGTH; seek his face always.
—1 Chronicles 16:11 (NIV)

Affirmation/prayer: Thank you, Lord, for the power of prayer and the strength you give me each day.

God is my source!

March 10

LOVE

We know how much God loves us, and we have put our trust in his love. God is love, and all who live in love live in God, and God lives in them.
—1 John 4:16 (NLT)

Affirmation/prayer: When I live in God, I live in love. In God's love I enjoy peace, happiness, joy, health, success, and contentment. In God's love I know what it means to love myself. In God's love I am able to form healthy relationships that are founded and rooted in love. God, help me to know that I am lovable and capable of giving and receiving love. Let nothing stop me from loving you and serving others.

God is my source!

March 11

GOD WITHIN

And let them make me a sanctuary; that I may dwell among them.
—Exodus 25:8 (NKV)

Do you not know that you are a temple of God and that the Spirit of God dwells in you.
—1 Corinthians 3:16 (NKV)

Affirmation/prayer: How awesome is that! God wants to be with me today. As a Christian all I need to connect with God in life is to look within my heart.

God is my source!

March 12

WAIT ON GOD

He gives strength to the weary and increases the power of the weak. Even youths grow tired and weary, and young men stumble and fall; but those who hope in the LORD will renew their strength. They will soar on wings like eagles; they will run and not grow weary, they will walk and not be faint.
—Isaiah 40:29–31 (NIV)

Affirmation/prayer: I will put my trust in God, and I will wait on him no matter what. Even when I say to myself, "I don't see how," I will still wait on God. In times past, waiting on you, Lord, has built my faith, courage, and endurance. The more I wait on the Lord, the easier it is for me to meet life's challenges. Lord, give me the patience to live in your strength and power. Give me the strength to wait on you.

God is my source!

March 13

ALL-KNOWING, EVER-PRESENT GOD

*I can never escape from your Spirit! I can never get away from
your presence! If I go up to heaven, you are there; if I go down to
the grave, you are there. If I ride the wings of the morning, if I
dwell by the farthest oceans, even there your hand will guide me,
and your strength will support me.*
—Psalms 139:7–10 (NLT)

Today, thank you, Lord, that whether I am at work, home, or
play, your spirit is always there. You see and know everything.
You strengthen and support me. I am can be faithful because
you are with me everywhere I go.

God is my source!

March 14

PROBLEMS

Cast all your anxiety on him because he cares for you.
—1 Peter 5:7 (NIV)

But if any of you lacks wisdom, let him ask of God, who gives to all generously and without reproach, and it will be given to him.
—James 1:5 (ESV)

Affirmation/prayer: There is no problem that God cannot solve. My problem is that I won't relinquish my self-control. The more problems I give to you, Lord, the more problems you will solve. You give me peace.

God is my source!

March 15

SATISFACTION

Jesus answered, "It is written: 'Man shall not live on bread alone, but on every word that comes from the mouth of God.'"
—Mathew 4:4 (NIV)

Affirmation/prayer: Today, thy word teaches me that it takes more than material possessions to satisfy. It is only God who can satisfy my needs completely.

God is my source!

March 16

MY HEART BELONGS TO GOD

God, create a pure heart in me, and renew a right attitude within me. Do not cast me from your presence; do not take your Holy Spirit from me. Restore to me the joy of your salvation, and let a willing attitude control me.
—Psalms 51:10–12 (ISV)

Affirmation/prayer: Giving my heart to God is the best decision I will make all day.

God is my source!

March 17

WHO AM I?

Guard your heart above all else, for it determines the course of your life.
—Proverbs 4:23 (NLT)

Affirmation/prayer: What I think of myself governs how I react with others. As I ask the question, "Who am I?" I open up to myself. Lord, please help me to discover my true inner being. Please show me how to align my inner thoughts with your will. To change the course of my life, I must look inside first!

God is my source!

March 18

POSITIVE THOUGHTS

Finally, brothers, whatever is true, whatever is honorable, whatever is just, whatever is pure, whatever is lovely, whatever is commendable, if there is any excellence, if there is anything worthy of praise, think about these things.
—Philippians 4:8 (NIV)

Affirmation/prayer: Negative thoughts about my problems will not foster positive changes in my life. Only positive thoughts have the power to heal my broken spirit and transform my life. Today I choose positive thoughts about where I am in life, my work, relationships, behavior, and my day. Instead of thinking on the negative, I will reflect on my blessings and give God the praise. Thank you, Lord, for your peace.

God is my source!

March 19

GOOD NEWS

Now, brothers and sisters, I want to remind you of the gospel I preached to you, which you received and on which you have taken your stand. By this gospel you are saved, if you hold firmly to the word I preached to you. Otherwise, you have believed in vain. For what I received I passed on to you as of first importance: that Christ died for our sins according to the Scriptures, that he was buried, that he was raised on the third day according to the Scriptures.

—1 Corinthians 15:1–4 (NIV)

Affirmation/prayer: Now that's the gospel, and it is Good News. Thanks to Jesus, I have eternal life.

God is my source!

March 20

TAKE RISKS

Farmers who wait for perfect weather never plant. If they watch every cloud, they never harvest.

Plant your seed in the morning and keep busy all afternoon, for you don't know if profit will come from one activity or another—or maybe both.
—Ecclesiastes 11:4, 6 (NLT)

Affirmation/prayer: I will not make excuses for not doing the things I need to do. Life is about change, and there are no guarantees of what today will bring. When I live in uncertainty and do not take risks, I will miss out on success. Lord, help me move past my fears and doubts of the past and do the things I need to do today. Give me your wisdom and knowledge of when to sow and when to reap. Give me the courage to take a healthy risk, even when I can't see the outcome.

God is my source!

March 21

REPEATING PROBLEMS

Then the disciples came to Jesus in private and asked, "Why couldn't we drive it out?" He replied, "Because you have so little faith. Truly I tell you, if you have faith as small as a mustard seed, you can say to this mountain, 'Move from here to there,' and it will move. Nothing will be impossible for you. But this kind does not go out except by prayer and fasting."
—Matthew 17:19–21 (NIV)

Affirmation/prayer: Although I may not have the kinds of demons there were in biblical times, I do have things that I deal with again and again. Things such as fear, doubt, bad habits, addictions, depression, and worldly cares continue to plague me. I can't conquer these problems solely on my own. Please, Lord Jesus, give me wisdom and knowledge from above. I will put my faith in You.

God is my source!

March 22

WHAT'S EATING AT YOU?

Let all bitterness, and wrath, and anger, and clamor, and evil speaking, be put away from you, with all malice: And be ye kind one to another, tenderhearted, forgiving one another, even as God for Christ's sake hath forgiven you.
—Ephesians 4:31–32 (ESV)

Affirmation/prayer: The things that are eating and destroying me within are bitterness, wrath, and anger. Shouting, cursing, saying evil, and doing malicious deeds are symptoms of what's eating at me within. Depression is often the cancer resulting from pent-up anger. When I am forgiving, kind, and tenderhearted, it is like medicine for my soul. Jesus, replace my faults with your spirit of peace, joy, love, kindness, and tender mercies. Thank you for loving and forgiving me.

God is my source!

March 23

TIME

This is the day which the Lord hath made; we will rejoice and be glad in it.
—Psalms 118:24 (NLT)

Affirmation/prayer: No matter how long I have lived or shall live, my life consists of one day at a time. Every day I wake up, I thank God for another day. Time is a gift that God has given me that is more precious than money, health, or strength. Dead men can't do what I can do today. Therefore, when I feel I have nothing to thank God for, I can thank him for one more day.

What shall I do with this day? I shall give God his portion and ask him how to use the rest. I will rejoice and be glad in it!

God is my source!

March 24

PEOPLE PLEASING

Fear of man will prove to be a snare whoever trusts in the Lord is kept safe.
—Proverbs 29:25 (NIV)

Affirmation/prayer: Fear sets in when pleasing people becomes my primary reason for living. Lord, help me control the ways I view and interact with people. You are God and they are not. Freedom and my blessings are waiting for me when I put God's will before the will of others.

God is my source!

March 25

IF IT BE THE LORD'S WILL

Come now, you who say, "Today or tomorrow we will go to such and such a city, spend a year there, buy and sell, and make a profit"; yet you do not know what tomorrow will bring. What is your life? For you are a mist that appears for a little time and then vanishes. Instead you ought to say, "If the Lord wills, we will live and do this or that."
—James 4:13–15 (ESV)

Affirmation/prayer: I used to say "I *am the master of my fate*: I *am* the *captain of my soul*."

This egotistic self-will is in contrast of the way God would have me to live. It forgets about God and puts me in control. Running my own ship has ruined many of my future plans. God's will is perfect. The Lord's will guides me and leads me to the good things of life. Lord, I seek your will. Lord, be the master of my fate, the captain of my soul.

God is my source!

March 26

HE NEVER FAILS

Then Jesus said to the twelve, "Do you also want to go away?" But Simon Peter answered Him, "Lord, to whom shall we go? You have the words of eternal life."
—John 6:67–68 (NKJV)

Affirmation/prayer: If I turn away from Jesus and his lead, where will I go? People, money, drugs, sex, alcohol, and all kinds of material possessions—all these have failed to bring anyone peace at one time or another. None will give me eternal life. Now I put my faith in Jesus Christ. He has never failed me yet.

God is my source!

March 27

RICH OR POOR

Keep falsehood and lies far from me; give me neither poverty nor riches, but give me only my daily bread. For if I grow rich, I may deny you and say, "Who is the LORD?" And if I am too poor, I may steal and thus insult God's holy name.
—Proverbs 30:8–9 (NASB)

But my God shall supply all your need according to his riches in glory by Christ Jesus.
—Philippians 4:19 (KJV)

Affirmation/prayer: I do not want to live a life of a helpless victim, one with a poverty mind-set. Nor do I want to live a life where my value and self-worth is based on how much I own. Therefore, I will be open to all the riches God has in store for me to receive. Rich or poor, I will remember:

God is my source!

March 28

STAND FIRM

If you do not stand firm in your faith, then you will not stand at all.
—Isaiah 7:9 (NIV)

For the LORD your God is living among you. He is a mighty savior. He will take delight in you with gladness. With his love, he will calm all your fears. He will rejoice over you with joyful songs.
—Zephaniah 3:17 (NLT)

Affirmation/prayer: Teach me, Lord, how to stand firm in my faith. Help me remember at all times that you are my friend not my enemy. Lord Jesus, faith in You is absolutely necessary to quiet and compose my mind during trials. Faith calms my fears. In you I can find love, peace, and eternal life. If I do not stand firm in my faith, then I will not stand at all.

God is my source!

March 29

A NEW WEEK

He gives power to the weak and strength to the powerless. Even youths will become weak and tired, and young men will fall in exhaustion. But those who trust in the LORD will find new strength. They will soar high on wings like eagles. They will run and not grow weary. They will walk and not faint.
—Isaiah 40:29–31 (NLT)

Affirmation/prayer: As I face a new week with its challenges, your word reminds me that I am only human. Lord, may I trust in you another week for my strength.

God is my source!

March 30

GOD LOVES ME

Let the morning bring me word of your unfailing love, for I have put my trust in you. Show me the way I should go, for to you I entrust my life.
—Psalms 143:8 (NIV)

Affirmation/prayer: God, may I hear your voice each and every morning. I know that you love me and will keep me on the right path. Without it I will run in circles listening to everyone else. Your love tenderly guides me because it wants what is best for me. Thank you, Lord, for loving me.

God is my source!

March 31

GRACE

I was given a thorn in my flesh, a messenger of Satan, to torment me. Three times I pleaded with the Lord to take it away from me. But he said to me, "My grace is sufficient for you, for my power is made perfect in weakness." Therefore, I will boast all the more gladly about my weaknesses, so that Christ's power may rest on me.
—2 Corinthians 12:7-9 (NIV)

Affirmation/prayer: Sometimes God's grace seems so far away from me. It is in these times I must remember that the grace that saved me before is still there and will be revealed in God's time, not as a result of anything I do or fail to do. His is grace is enough for me.

God is my source!

April

April 1

MY BLESSINGS

Bless the LORD, O my soul, and all that is within me, bless his holy name! Bless the LORD, O my soul, and forget not all his benefits, who forgives all your iniquity, who heals all your diseases, who redeems your life from the pit, who crowns you with steadfast love and mercy.
—Psalms 103:1–4 (ESV)

Affirmation/prayer: God the Father heals me, forgives me, comforts me, loves me, gives me his best.

He is good to me.

God is my source!

April 2

THE VISION

For still the vision awaits its appointed time; it hastens to the end—it will not lie. If it seems slow, wait for it; it will surely come; it will not delay.
—Habakkuk 2:3 (ESV)

Affirmation/prayer: I have many goals and visions for my life. I will align my goals, visions, and expectations with God's vision for me. If I lose heart or become impatient, I will turn to his word to remind me that when things are not headed in the direction that I want them to, good things will surely come when I wait and trust God.

God is my source!

April 3

WISDOM

The fear of the LORD is the beginning of knowledge: but fools despise wisdom and instruction.
—Proverbs 1:7 (NIV)

The way to become wise is to honor the LORD; he gives sound judgment to all who obey his commands. He is to be praised forever.
—Psalms 111:10 (GNT)

For the wisdom of this world is foolishness to God. As the Scriptures say, "He traps the wise in the snare of their own cleverness."
—1 Corinthians 3:19 (NLT)

Affirmation/prayer: No matter how much knowledge I have, my wisdom is nothing compared to God's wisdom. If I align my purpose for living with what the world says, I will miss out on my true purpose for living. I become wise when I recognize that my thinking is limited and powerless to control my life, much less the lives of other people. I will relax and be patient as I live a life not from the world's perspective but by God's wisdom. Lord, teach me how to stay close to you, my fountain of wisdom.

God is my source!

April 4

GOD DELIVERS

We were under great pressure, far beyond our ability to endure, so that we despaired of life itself. Indeed, we felt we had received the sentence of death. But this happened that we might not rely on ourselves but on God, who raises the dead. He has delivered us from such a deadly peril, and he will deliver us again. On him we have set our hope that he will continue to deliver us, as you help us by your prayers.
—2 Corinthians 1:8–11 (NIV)

Affirmation/prayer: Life got you down? Remember this: he has delivered. He is delivering. He will deliver.

God is my source!

April 5

LOVE OF MONEY

Every good and perfect gift is from above, coming down from the Father of the heavenly lights, who does not change like shifting shadows.
—James 1:17 (NIV)

I left my mother's womb naked, and I will return to God naked. The LORD has given, and the LORD has taken. May the name of the LORD be blessed.
—Job 1:21 (ISV)

For the love of money is a root of all kinds of evil. Some people, eager for money, have wandered from the faith and pierced themselves with many griefs.
—1 Timothy 6:10 (NIV)

Affirmation/prayer: Jesus, when I consider all the things that I own, my most precious gift is a relationship with you. Please don't let the love of money or any other thing cloud this reality. When I take my eyes off you and pursue money, grief is not fall behind. I was born, this world already created by you. I have nothing to offer to creation. No matter how much money you give me, I still can't take it with me. Jesus keep my heart and do not let me leave you because of my love of money.

God is my source!

April 6

CONSISTENCY

Jesus Christ is the same yesterday and today and forever.
—Hebrews 13:8 (NIV)

We have this hope as an anchor for the soul, firm and secure. It enters the inner sanctuary behind the curtain, where our forerunner, Jesus, has entered on our behalf. He has become a high priest forever in the order of Melchizedek.
—Hebrews 6:19–20 (NIV)

Affirmation/prayer: Jesus, your love, compassion, care, and empathy is always consistent.

You are the center of my life.
You are the one I should follow.
You are the one to share with others.
You are the one I can count on.
Why? Because no matter what I experience, you are my anchor.

God, you are my source!

April 7

BE STILL

He says, "Be still, and know that I am God…"
—Psalms 46:10

Be thou exalted, LORD, in thine own strength: so will we sing and praise thy power.
—Psalms 21:13

Affirmation/prayer: When I slow down and think about God and his mighty power, I know that he is capable of addressing the things that I care about in this life. Not by my strength, Lord, but by our strength I will live my life. Lord, you are God and know what is best for me and those around me. Teach me how to pray and meditate on your word. Teach me how to slow down and wait on you.

God is my source!

April 8

OVERCOMING HARD TIMES

Blessed is the man who remains steadfast under trial, for when he has stood the test he will receive the crown of life, which God has promised to those who love him.
—James 1:12 (ESV)

Affirmation/prayer: Today, I know that hard times are just part of life. When I am going through hard times, Lord, remind me that if I can keep the faith, all will be well. These times may be just what I need to get me just where I need to be. May my hard times teach me the skills that I need to grow and to be an overcomer. When my trials are over, if I keep the faith, not only will life on earth be better, but I can also look forward to eternal life in Jesus. Therefore, I will remember that even during the hard times,

God is my source!

April 9

TEARS

You know how troubled I am; you have kept a record of my tears. Aren't they listed in your book? 9. The day I call to you, my enemies will be turned back. I know this: God is on my side.
—Psalms 56:8–9 (GNT)

He will wipe every tear from their eyes. There will be no more death or mourning or crying or pain, for the old order of things has passed away.
—Revelation 21:4 (NIV)

Jesus wept.
—John 11:35 (NIV)

Affirmation/prayer: Others may not know, but God sees me every time I cry. Each tear I shed means something to God. His word tells me He is tenderhearted and shares with me and weeps with me. God loves me.

God is my source!

April 10

WHY?

A person's steps are directed by the LORD. How then can anyone understand their own way.
—Proverbs 20:24 (NIV)

Trust in the LORD with all your heart; do not depend on your own understanding. Seek his will in all you do, and he will show you which path to take.
—Proverbs 3:5–6 (NLT)

Affirmation/prayer: Even though God has given me free will to choose my actions, I don't have control over the consequences. When I do things my way, I am often left saying, "Why, Lord, did it not work out?" Lord, even when I think I understand, I still need you to show me the way to go. May I trust and follow you. Thank you for ordering my steps.

God is my source!

April 11

GOD'S COUNSEL

I will bless the LORD who counsels me—even at night when my thoughts trouble me (CSB). I will always look to you, as you stand beside me and protect me from fear. With all my heart, I will celebrate, and I can safely rest. (CEV)

You have shown me the path to life, and you make me glad by being near to me. Sitting at your right side, I will always be joyful. —Psalms 16:7–9, 11 (CEV)

Affirmation/prayer: Thank you, Lord, for your word that instructs me in my deepest thoughts. Some of my best counsel and ideas come to me at night. You give me sweet rest by removing worry, evil thoughts, and regrets. You are always there to counsel me, even subconsciously, through a song or scripture. May I think of you in my darkest hour. Your word gives me sweet peace.

God is my source!

April 12

HIS WORD

The rain and snow come down from the heavens and stay on the ground to water the earth. They cause the grain to grow, producing seed for the farmer and bread for the hungry. It is the same with my word. I send it out, and it always produces fruit. It will accomplish all I want it to, and it will prosper everywhere I send it.
—Isaiah 55:10–11 (NLT)

The grass withers and the flowers fade, but the word of our God stands forever.
—Isaiah 40:8 (NLT)

Affirmation/prayer: Living in a world where people's conversations can be superficial or phony, it is good to know that I can depend on what God says. As I read your word, may it grow in my heart and flourish. Please, Jesus, speak to my heart as I read the word so that it will accomplish its purpose in my life.

God is my source!

April 13

PROCRASTINATION

All hard work brings a profit, but mere talk leads only to poverty.
—Proverbs 14:23 (NIV)

Do not boast about tomorrow, for you do not know what a day may bring.
—Proverbs 27:1 (NIV)

Lazy hands make for poverty but diligent hands bring wealth.
—Proverbs 10:4 (NIV)

Affirmation/prayer: Lord, you have a plan for my life, and it does not include procrastination. Please do not let me procrastinate, but keep me on track pertaining to your will. Give me the courage to face the things that I do not want to do today. Let me be not only a talker but a doer of your word. You have many blessings for me today, and if I procrastinate, it may be too late for me to receive them tomorrow. This is especially true when it comes down to my salvation. Thank you for all of your many blessings, as you keep me on track and continually encourage me to work diligently, no matter what.

God is my source!

April 14

HE KNOWS AND UNDERSTANDS

For we do not have a high priest who is unable to empathize with our weaknesses, but we have one who has been tempted in every way, just as we are—yet he did not sin. Let us then approach God's throne of grace with confidence, so that we may receive mercy and find grace to help us in our time of need.
—Hebrews 4:15–16 (NIV)

Affirmation/prayer: Oh, how wonderful to talk to a friend who has experienced what you are going through! Jesus, you say to me in the midst of my struggles, tears, and sorrows, "I have been there too." You say to me, "I also have been down this road before, and I understand what you are going through." You have been tempted as I am tempted. Thank you that you conquered all so that I can come to you to find empathy, help, grace, and mercy. Thank you, Jesus, for loving me.

God is my source!

April 15

I AM NOT ALONE

So do not fear, for I am with you; do not be dismayed, for I am your God. I will strengthen you and help you; I will uphold you with my righteous right hand.
—Isaiah 41:10 (NIV)

What then shall we say in response to these things? If God is for us, who can be against us?
—Romans 8:31 (NIV)

Affirmation/prayer: Oh, how good it is to know that I do not have to go through life alone! When I think of the many blessings of the past, I know that God is faithful. God, I know you are able to help me carry the load. Help me stand firm in the faith so that fear and doubt will not toss me about like the waves of an ocean. Lord, be with me and take all my strains and stresses. If you are with me, who can be against me?

God is my source!

April 16

WELLS

When the LORD your God brings you into the land he swore to your fathers, to Abraham, Isaac and Jacob, to give you—a land with large, flourishing cities you did not build, houses filled with all kinds of good things you did not provide, wells you did not dig, and vineyards and olive groves you did not plant—then when you eat and are satisfied, be careful that you do not forget the LORD.
—Deuteronomy 6:10–12 (NIV)

Affirmation/prayer: Thy word teaches me to be thankful. Thank you, Lord, for my family, friends, and strangers who were kind enough to dig the wells that I have drunk from. Wells of wisdom, knowledge, and blessings that I did not dig but gave me drink when I was thirsty. I will not forget to dig my own wells of kindness in which others may drink. Thank you Lord all that you have given through the hands of others.

God is my source!

April 17

MY STRENGTH

Hear my cry, O God; Give heed to my prayer. From the end of the earth I call to You when my heart is faint; Lead me to the rock that is higher than I. For You have been a refuge for me, A tower of strength against the enemy.
—Psalms 61:1–3 (NASB)

Do not be grieved, for the joy of the LORD is your strength.
—Nehemiah 8:10 (NIV)

Affirmation/prayer: It is okay to admit that there are some cares and troubles in this world that are too big for me to handle alone. It is also okay to pray to God for my strength when I am too weak to face life problems. I am not be afraid to face my problems because my dependence on God is the beginning of my strength and the end of my weaknesses.

God is my source!

April 18

YESTERDAY'S FAILURES

That is why, for Christ's sake, I delight in weaknesses, in insults, in hardships, in persecutions, in difficulties. For when I am weak, then I am strong.
—2 Corinthians 12:10 (NIV)

Affirmation/prayer: Thank God for his grace that gives me the strength to move on. I won't let yesterday's failures weigh me down!

God is my source!

April 19

CHANGE

Forget the former things; do not dwell on the past. See, I am doing a new thing! Now it springs up; do you not perceive it? I am making a way in the wilderness and streams in the wasteland.
—Isaiah 43:18–19 (NIV)

Brothers and sisters, I do not consider myself yet to have taken hold of it. But one thing I do: Forgetting what is behind and straining toward what is ahead.
—Philippians 3:13 (NIV)

Affirmation/prayer: I can't change the past, so I will not dwell on it. The secret of a better life is to focus on today's blessings instead of wasting my time and energy focusing on the past. God has in store for me new and better things. Lord, help me seize the new opportunities that you send my way today. Please give me the fortitude to use these opportunities to build a better and brighter future.

God is my source!

April 20

JOY

I have told you these things so that you will be filled with my joy. Yes, your joy will overflow!
—John 15:11 (NLT)

May the God of hope fill you with all joy and peace as you trust in him, so that you may overflow with hope by the power of the Holy Spirit.
—Romans 15:13 (NIV)

Affirmation/prayer: Knowing that Jesus loves me gives me joy. I can't find this kind of complete joy in any other person or thing. The world says, "Get this or that, and you will be happy." The world's joy comes from without, but God-given joy lives deep within and overflows outward. Thank you for a joy that is greater than my circumstances. Jesus, remind me to trust in you every day, not just for things to make me happy but for an overflowing joy that gives me hope.

God is my source!

April 21

LIVING TODAY

But more than anything else, put God's work first and do what he wants. Then the other things will be yours as well. Don't worry about tomorrow. It will take care of itself. You have enough to worry about today.
—Matthew 6:33–34 (CEV)

Affirmation/prayer: When I wake up in the morning and pray and ask God to use me, I am putting God in the lead. Knowing that I am working for God and not man gives me peace. Good things happen when I put God first. When I work for God, he gives me strength to overcome procrastination and fear. Learning he is with me now today lets me know he will be with me tomorrow. Putting God first removes worry about tomorrow and helps me live one day at a time.

Lord, thank you for this day.

God is my source!

April 22

GIVE YOURSELF CREDIT

The LORD does not look at the things people look at. People look at the outward appearance, but the LORD looks at the heart.
—1 Samuel 16:7 (NIV)

I can do all this through him who gives me strength.
—Philippians 4:13 (NIV)

Affirmation/prayer: It is me and not God who is constantly comparing myself to others. It is me and not God who is constantly criticizing myself and putting myself down. God does not see my outward appearance as man sees me. God sees my body, my spirit, and my soul.

Today I will treat myself and love myself as God loves me. Each time I am aware of the tendency to compare myself to others and put myself down, I will affirm through God's word who I am and whose I am. I am a beautiful child of God who deserves to be respected and loved.

God is my source!

April 23

MY DAILY BREAD

Give us this day our daily bread.
—Matthew 6:11 (NIV)

Affirmation/prayer: Lord, nourish me today spiritually, physically, mentally, and emotionally. As I put my trust in you, remove all worry and doubt about today. May I not live a life that is self-sufficient but one that looks to you for everything that I need. Give me this day my daily bread.

God is my source!

April 24

DO RIGHT

For we are taking pains to do what is right, not only in the eyes of the Lord but also in the eyes of man.
—2 Corinthians 8:21 (NIV)

Affirmation/prayer: God, please direct my thinking so that my actions are not motivated by hate, jealousy, greed, or power. In all that I do, may I have a good conscience in your sight. Give me the wisdom and knowledge to treat others the way you would have me treat them. In all of this, build my character so that I will be pleasing to you and all those that you would have me to serve. Give me the strength to do the right thing.

God is my source!

April 25

MY STRENGTH

He gives power to the weak and strength to the powerless. Even youths will become weak and tired, and young men will fall in exhaustion. But those who trust in the LORD will find new strength. They will soar high on wings like eagles. They will run and not grow weary. They will walk and not faint.
—Isaiah 40:29–31 (NLT)

Affirmation/prayer: As I face a new week with its challenges, your word reminds me that I am only human. Lord, may I trust in you another week for my strength.

God is my source!

April 26

LET GO AND LET GOD

I pray that out of his glorious riches he may strengthen you with power through his Spirit in your inner being.

Now to him who is able to do immeasurably more than all we ask or imagine, according to his power that is at work within us. To him be glory in the church and in Christ Jesus throughout all generations, for ever and ever! Amen.
—Ephesians 3:16, 20–21 (NIV)

Affirmation/prayer: I will never live this life to the point that I do not need to ask God for his strength. Lord, I ask for your spirit to strengthen me so that I may live a life beyond my limited abilities. Help me tune into your inner spirit, for everything good in me comes from above, things more than I can imagine. To you, Lord, who is more than able to provide more than I can ask, think, or imagine, I ask for grace, peace, courage, and the strength to let go of self and completely trust in you in all that I do.

God is my source!

April 27

CONQUERING FEAR

Don't be afraid, for I am with you. Don't be discouraged, for I am your God. I will strengthen you and help you. I will hold you up with my victorious right hand.
—Isaiah 41:10 (NLT)

Affirmation/prayer: Because of human nature, there will always be times that I am fearful. When fear sets in, I will remember that God is present with me. Lord, help me to remember that you are my strength. Give me the faith to trust in you and not fear so that I will not be discouraged. God, you are holding my hand, so there is nothing that I should fear because you are with me.

God, you are my strength! I will not be afraid!

God is my source!

April 28

PEACE WITHIN

"I have told you these things, so that in me you may have peace. In this world you will have trouble. But take heart! I have overcome the world."
—John 16:33 (NIV)

Affirmation/prayer: Jesus, when I look outside of me to find peace in things or people, I find no lasting peace. If I am not at peace with myself, there is no peace. Lasting peace I find within as I connect with you, Jesus. I give you my fears and doubts. Take my hand and lead me down your path of joy and peace within.

God is my source!

April 29

WANT TO BE HAPPY?

Always be joyful. Never stop praying. Be thankful in all circumstances, for this is God's will for you who belong to Christ Jesus. Do not stifle the Holy Spirit.
—1 Thessalonians 5:16–19 (NLT)

Affirmation/prayer: No matter the situation, I will choose to be happy every day. I choose to be happy by calming my anxious thoughts through prayer and meditation. I pray for God to fill me with his joy. I choose to be happy by taking my eyes off all that is wrong and thanking Jesus for all that is good. I choose to be happy by opening my eyes to the spirit that shines within. Thank you, Jesus, that today and always I can choose to be happy.

God is my source!

April 30

PATIENCE AND PERSISTENCE

Be patient, then, brothers and sisters, until the Lord's coming. See how the farmer waits for the land to yield its valuable crop, patiently waiting for the autumn and spring rains. You, too, must be patient. Take courage, for the coming of the Lord is near.
—James 5:7 (NIV)

Affirmation/prayer: There will be many seasons in my life. When I don't attain my goals as quickly as I want, or when I want, I become discouraged. Lord, grant me the courage to keep on going, knowing that things of value such as character, love, faith, and hope take time to grow.

God is my source!

May

May 1

YOU CAN'T BUY LOVE

Love is patient, love is kind. It does not envy, it does not boast, it is not proud.

It always protects, always trusts, always hopes, always perseveres. Love never fails.
—1 Corinthians 13:4, 7–8 (NIV)

Many waters cannot quench love, neither can the floods drown it: if a man would give all the wealth of his house for love, it would utterly be rejected.
—Song of Solomon 8:7(KJ2000)

Affirmation/prayer: People who love you because of wealth or prestige will reject you when it is gone. True love has no price. Thank you, Lord, for your gift of love (John 3:16). Thank you for those who truly love me.

God is my source!

May 2

WISDOM

If you are wise and understand God's ways, prove it by living an honorable life, doing good works with the humility that comes from wisdom. But if you are bitterly jealous and there is selfish ambition in your heart, don't cover up the truth with boasting and lying. For jealousy and selfishness are not God's kind of wisdom. Such things are earthly, unspiritual, and demonic.

But the wisdom from above is first of all pure. It is also peace loving, gentle at all times, and willing to yield to others. It is full of mercy and the fruit of good deeds. It shows no favoritism and is always sincere.

And those who are peacemakers will plant seeds of peace and reap a harvest of righteousness.
—James 3:13–15, 17–18 (NLT)

Affirmation/prayer: I will look at how I treat God, myself, and others to determine whether I have been wise or foolish. I will truthfully examine my heart to discover the motives behind the things that I do. If I find that my actions have been the result of self-ambitions and jealousy, I will God for forgiveness and mercy. Lord, fill me with a wisdom from heaven that is pure; then I will be peace and love. Search my heart, Lord; I need your wisdom.

God is my source!

May 3

POSITIVE THOUGHTS

Finally, my friends, keep your minds on whatever is true, pure, right, holy, friendly, and proper. Don't ever stop thinking about what is truly worthwhile and worthy of praise.
—Philippians 4:8(CEV)

Affirmation/prayer: Lord, today help me keep my focus on you and your words. If I am to have positive thoughts, I must not spend time only thinking about things that are going wrong in my life. Instead, through prayer and meditation, I will give my thoughts to you, Jesus. Please help me see the good, worthwhile, and beautiful things around me. Help me get rid of selfishness and think about all of the good that I can do for others.

God is good.

God is my source!

May 4

LETTING GO OF FEAR

So do not fear, for I am with you; do not be dismayed, for I am your God. I will strengthen you and help you; I will uphold you with my righteous right hand.
—Isaiah 41:10 (NIV)

Affirmation/prayer: Lord Jesus, help me put my fears aside and embrace your strength. Gently take fear from me, and replace it with the feelings of peace and serenity. When fear arises because of old thought patterns, help me face fear, knowing that you will always protect me. You are holding my hand, so I can relax in problematic situations, knowing that things will turn out for my good. May my fears slip away, knowing that you are beside me and holding my right hand.

God is my source!

May 5

GETTING INTO SHAPE

"Go down to the potter's house, and there I will give you my message." So, I went down to the potter's house, and I saw him working at the wheel. But the pot he was shaping from the clay was marred in his hands; so the potter formed it into another pot, shaping it as seemed best to him. Then the word of the LORD came to me. He said, "Can I not do with you, Israel, as this potter does?" declares the LORD. "Like clay in the hand of the potter, so are you in my hand, Israel."
—Jeremiah 18:2–6 (NIV)

Affirmation/prayer: God has a plan and a will for my life. Oftentimes When I am in control.my life does not look like vessel that God had in mind. Like a marred vessel, I am in your hands to do with me as you please. I give you control to reshape me like the potter does to the clay into what you would have me to be. The more that I am shaped into your mold, the more my spirit and soul are lifted and healed. Like a new, shiny vessel, my life will be a reflection of your love, peace, and forgiveness.

Thank you, Lord, that you are the Potter and I am your clay!

God is my source!

May 6

HE NEVER LEAVES ME

Once I was young, and now I am old. Yet I have never seen the godly abandoned or their children begging for bread. They are always generous and lend freely; their children will be a blessing. Turn from evil and do good; then you will dwell in the land forever.

—Psalms 37:25–27 (NIV)

Affirmation/prayer: It is not always easy to do good and not evil in our society today. Lord, as your child, may my thoughts and ways even in the smallest decisions be to do what is right and good in your sight (your will). May my life be a blessing and witness to my children and others of your faithfulness, goodness, and mercy. Jesus never leaves or forsakes his children. Amen!

God is my source!

May 7

THE LOVE OF MONEY

Keep your lives free from the love of money and be content with what you have, because God has said, "Never will I leave you; never will I forsake you." So, we say with confidence, "The Lord is my helper; I will not be afraid. What can mere mortals do to me?"
—Hebrews 13:5–6 (NIV)

Affirmation/prayer: Money comes and money goes! The one thing in life I know that is consistent is that God that will never leave me or forsake me. Lord, help me view and use wisely the money you have so freely given me. I pray that I always remember that faith in you, not man or money, will give me the lasting peace and contentment I desire.

God is my source!

May 8

SEEK PEACE

Turn away from evil and do good. Search for peace, and work to maintain it.
—1 Peter 3:11 (NLT)

Do all that you can to live in peace with everyone.
—Romans 12:18 (NLT)

Affirmation/prayer: Lord, help me to examine my ways to see if I am a peace seeker. Keep my heart from malicious thoughts and actions so that I may maintain peace in all my relationships. As I seek peace through meditation and prayer, comfort me and show me how to live a life of peace. Peace does not always come easy, but I know, dear Lord, that if I do my part, you will give me the peace of mind that I so desire. Thank you, Lord, for your peace.

God is my source!

May 9

THE LIGHT

The LORD is my light and my salvation; whom shall I fear? the LORD is the strength of my life; of whom shall I be afraid?
—Psalms 27:1 (ISV)

Affirmation/prayer: "The Lord is my light and my salvation." I have all the light I need for today. When I am afraid of dark times, the Lord will give me his light. His light is my courage and my strength. When I am lost and don't know where to go or what to do, I humbly ask you, Lord, to continue to let your light guide me and show me the way to go. I can face my fears head-on knowing that God is in charge. He is my light of my life. He is not very far away.

God is the light of my life!

God is my source!

May 10

CLAIMING MY DESTINY

If they had been thinking of the country they had left, they would have had opportunity to return. Instead, they were longing for a better country—a heavenly one. Therefore, God is not ashamed to be called their God, for he has prepared a city for them.
—Hebrews 11:15–16 (NIV)

Affirmation/prayer: Am I letting go of my destiny by holding on to my history? Forget about it and move on! Thank you, Lord, for the wonderful things you have prepared for me to receive. I just need to keep moving forward and not look back.

God is my source of good things to come!

May 11

PEACE

I have told you these things, so that in me you may have peace. In this world you will have trouble. But take heart! I have overcome the world.
—John 16:33 (NIV)

Affirmation/prayer: Lord Jesus, please shine peace in my troubled heart and mind. Lift me above my circumstances. Give me guidance and clear direction. Give me the rest, peace, and joy that no one can take from me.

God is my source!

May 12

GOOD GIFTS

Our people must learn to devote themselves to doing what is good, in order to provide for urgent needs and not live unproductive lives.
—Titus 3:14 (NIV)

Affirmation/prayer: All my blessings are gifts from God. What I do with these blessings, however, is my choice. Your word encourages me to work hard to help other people. Give me the wisdom and strength to know when and how to give good gifts that honor you. The most satisfying life I can live is a life that serves you by helping others. May thy will be done on earth as it is in heaven.

God is my source!

May 13

LETTING GO OF CHAOS AND CONFUSION

For God is not a God of disorder but of peace…
—1 Corinthians 14:33 (NLT)

Think over what I say, for the Lord will give you understanding in everything.
—2 Timothy 2:7 (NLT)

Affirmation/prayer: When the way is not clear and my mind is clouded and confused, I know this feeling is not from God. The best way to have clarity is to stop, rest, pray, and wait on God. God operates in the realm of my peace of mind. The only way that I can remove chaos and confusion and replace it with peace is to trust God. Lord, I give to you all chaos and confusion that I have created. I humbly ask that you replace it with your peace.

God is my source!

May 14

MY CUP

You treat me to a feast, while my enemies watch. You honor me as your guest, and you fill my cup until it overflows.
—Psalms 23:5 (CEV)

Affirmation/prayer: Lord, fill my cup. When I let others fill my cup, I get all sorts of things in my cup. Besides, no one else is responsible to fill my cup. Lord, fill my cup with love, joy, peace, patience, kindness, goodness, faithfulness, gentleness, and self-control. When you fill my cup I am blessed. Lord, fill my cup!

God is my source!

May 15

I SEE YOUR JOY

Let all that I am praise the LORD; may I never forget the good things he does for me.
—Psalms 103:2 (NLT)

Affirmation/prayer: What I am does indeed speak louder than what I say. I will rejoice in the Lord, not only in words but deeds. My family and friends will see my love for God by what I do and say in my going about the everyday business of living. They will know that I am his child by the kind deeds I do.

God is my source!

May 16

SHADOW OF HIS WINGS

Because you are my helper, I sing for joy in the shadow of your wings. I cling to you; your strong right hand holds me securely.
—Psalms 63:7–8 (NLT)

Affirmation/prayer: I sing for joy because everything that I need shall be provided today. When I live in the shadow of his wings, even if I don't always know what I need, God does. God is my helper and strength.

God is my source!

May 17

WISDOM BRINGS HAPPINESS

Happy is the man who finds wisdom, And the man who gains understanding.
—Proverbs 3:13 (NKJV)

She [wisdom] is *a tree of life to those who take hold of her, And happy* are all *who retain her.*
—Proverbs 3:18 (NKJV)

Affirmation/prayer: Wisdom makes me happy by showing me the way to live, helping me solve my problems, comforting me, and giving me a long life. It is my choice to be wise or foolish. Lord, slow me down and calm my thoughts today so that I may get a good understanding in all I do. Make me wise and happy.

God is my source!

May 18

TALK ABOUT IT

Don't worry about anything; instead, pray about everything. Tell God what you need, and thank him for all he has done. Then you will experience God's peace, which exceeds anything we can understand.
—Philippians 4:6–7(NLT)

But in my distress, I cried out to the LORD; yes, I prayed to my God for help. He heard me from his sanctuary; my cry to him reached his ears.
—Psalms 18:6 (NLT)

Affirmation/prayer: Jesus, if I am fearful, lonely, mad, jealous, proud, sexually immoral, gossiping, deceitful, blessed, or any state, you already know about it. When I pray and confess my faults, it is a reality check for me and not You. Lord, help me overcome anything that separates me from you. Jesus, please hear my prayer, forgive me for my sins, and refresh my spirit.

God is my source!

May 19

GOD INCLUDED

We may think we are doing the right thing, but the LORD always knows what is in our hearts.
—Proverbs 21:2 (CEV)

I know, LORD, that we humans are not in control of our own lives.
—Jeremiah 10:23 (CEV)

Affirmation/prayer: Despite reading many books and programs about how to improve myself, I have failed to do so when God was not part of the plan. Only with the help of God have I seen lasting improvement. God, help me include your word and the guidance of the Holy Spirit in all I do.

God is my source!

May 20

GOD HATES

There are six things the LORD hates—no, seven things he detests: haughty (proud) eyes, a lying tongue, hands that shed innocent blood,

a heart that devises wicked schemes, feet that are quick to rush into evil, a false witness who pours out lies and a person who stirs up conflict in the community.
—Proverbs 6:16–19 (NIV)

Affirmation/prayer: These are the things that God hates. Thank God that he loves me enough to give me his word so that I may know how to live a life that honors him. Thank God for his Holy Spirit, mercy, and grace that helps me do just that. Lord, help me to stay away from the things you hate.

God is my source!

May 21

PATIENCE, EXPERIENCE, AND HOPE

We can rejoice, too, when we run into problems and trials, for we know that they help us develop endurance. And endurance develops strength of character, and character strengthens our confident hope of salvation.
—Romans 5:3–4 (NLT)

Affirmation/prayer: When I look back, I can actually praise God for many of the problems that I have faced in life. It is through these problems that I have gained patience, experience, and hope. God-given patience tells me to wait on God. Experience tells me that the answer is out there and will come in its due time. It is hope that fills me with confidence and expectation to hold on, knowing that God has answered my prayers in the past and will do so again in the future. Thank you, Lord, for my trials that have given me patience, experiences, and hope.

God is my source!

May 22

A CHILDLIKE SPIRIT

My heart is not proud, Lord, my eyes are not haughty; I do not concern myself with great matters. or things too wonderful for me. But I have calmed and quieted myself, I am like a weaned child with its mother; like a weaned child I am content. Israel, put your hope in the LORD both now and forevermore.
—Psalms 131:1–3 (NIV)

Affirmation/prayer: Lord, today when I am tempted to get upset, I will calm my spirit by releasing to you my fears, worry, ego, and pride. Your word teaches me that I can always put my trust in you as a small child trusts his mother.

God is my source!

May 23

DEPENDENCY

But he said to me, "My grace is sufficient for you, for my power is made perfect in weakness." Therefore I will boast all the more gladly about my weaknesses, so that Christ's power may rest on me.
—2 Corinthians 12:9 (NIV)

Affirmation/prayer: It is in true humility that I feel and confess that I am human and I have my own weaknesses. Lord, I open my heart and ask that you lift me up with your power and your strength. I cannot make it by myself. I recognize that if it were not for your grace and mercy that refreshes me and lifts me up, I would not have the strength to go on. May your strength that lives in me be seen by others. Thank you, Lord, for my weaknesses, for it is when I am weak that your strength show up in me and makes me strong.

God is my source!

May 24

GOD BLESS AMERICA

I urge, then, first of all, that petitions, prayers, intercession and thanksgiving be made for all people—for kings and all those in authority [president, Congress, Senate, judges, police officers, etc.

] *that we may live peaceful and quiet lives in all godliness and holiness.*
—1 Timothy 2:1–2 (NIV)

Affirmation/prayer: Thank you, Lord, for the power of prayer. My prayer today is for my family, my friends, and my country. May you guide us in the way of peace.

God bless America!

God is my source!

May 25

MY COUNSELOR

I was foolish and ignorant; Yet I still belong to you; you hold my right hand. You guide me with your counsel, leading me to a glorious destiny. Whom have I in heaven but you? I desire you more than anything on earth. My health may fail, and my spirit may grow weak, but God remains the strength of my heart; he is mine forever.
—Psalms 73:22–26 (NLT)

And he will be called Wonderful Counselor, Mighty God, Everlasting Father, Prince of Peace.
—Isaiah 9:6 (NLT)

Affirmation/prayer: Jesus, I thank you for your words of wisdom that counsel me and keep me on the right path. Although the counsel of man may fail me, I know that I can depend on thee. There is no other person or thing that I can rely on that will not fail me. I know you will never leave me. I have an everlasting confidence that no matter what problems I face, you are there to lead and guide me. Praise you, Lord, for you are my Wonderful Counselor, Mighty God, Everlasting Father, and Prince of Peace. Amen.

God is my source!

May 26

THE GIFT OF PEACE

Now may the Lord of peace himself give you peace at all times and in every way. The Lord be with all of you.
—2 Thessalonians 3:16 (NLT)

And the peace of God, which transcends all understanding, will guard your hearts and your minds in Christ Jesus.
—Philippians 4:7 (NIV)

Affirmation/prayer: Dear God I am grateful for your gift of peace. Staying in contact with your peace daily helps me to take the most difficult circumstances in stride. Now things that once sent me into a nosedive are under my control. May I continue to grow in your peace.

God is my source!

May 27

"DON'T WORRY, BE HAPPY"

Don't worry and ask yourselves, "Will we have anything to eat? Will we have anything to drink? Will we have any clothes to wear?" Only people who don't know God are always worrying about such things. Your Father in heaven knows you need all of these. But more than anything else, put God's work first and do what he wants. Then the other things will be yours as well.
—Matthew 6:31–33 (CEV)

Affirmation/prayer: Without God I worry about other people. I worry about me. I worry about work. If God does not come first, everything else suffers.

God, help me to remember that. God must come first. God is my number one priority. God will provide; therefore, I will enjoy life and be happy!

God is my source!

May 28

MY JOY

You are from God, little children, and have overcome them; because greater is He who is in you than he who is in the world.
—1 John 4:4 (NASB)

Affirmation/prayer: I give thanks daily to God that his divine revealed word gives me all that I need to maintain the course and finish the race. My joy remains in this, that greater is he that is in me than he that is in the world.

God is my source!

May 29

BROKENHEARTED

He heals the brokenhearted and bandages their wounds.
—Psalms 147:3 (NLT)

The LORD is close to the brokenhearted and saves those who are crushed in spirit.
—Psalms 34:18 (NIV)

Affirmation/prayer: Having many problems to deal with in this world will sometimes leave me heartbroken, disappointed, or even grief stricken. It is at this time that I can depend on you, God, to cover my broken heart with your love. When my heart breaks, Jesus, you are the first to know. Bandage and heal anything in me that is broken. Thank you for your healing power that restores me when I am down. Lord Jesus, I feel your love every day. I will say to myself, "Cheer up. Feelings don't last always. Every road comes to an end." Put your trust in God.

God is my source!

May 30

THE VISION

Then the LORD told me: "I will give you my message in the form of a vision. Write it clearly enough to be read at a glance. At the time I have decided, my words will come true. You can trust what I say about the future. It may take a long time, but keep on waiting—it will happen!"
—Habakkuk 2:2–4 (CEV)

For as he thinketh in his heart, so is he.
—Proverbs 23:7 (NKJV)

Affirmation/prayer: Lord, when you put a dream in my heart, help me wait on you. I will take the time to think about and write down my goals. I know that there is power in visualization. Help me do things to keep the vision alive. Pictures and goals on my vision board will keep me focused. My theme will be that God is the center of my universe. Happy thoughts of things to come—I will work and wait on the appointed time for each and every dream. When my goals are God's will, I can trust that God will make them come true.

God is my source!

May 31

WHY BOAST?

This is what the LORD says: "Let not the wise boast of their wisdom or the strong boast of their strength or the rich boast of their riches.

But let the one who boasts boast about this: that they have the understanding to know me, that I am the LORD, who exercises kindness, justice and righteousness on earth, for in these I delight," declares the LORD.
—Jeremiah 9:23–24 (NIV)

Affirmation/prayer: Lord, all that I am is because of you. Help me beware to not boast of self or stuff, but boast of your justice, kindness, love, and mercy, which you freely give daily to your children.

God is my source!

June

.

June 1

THOUGHTS

To focus our minds on the human nature leads to death, but to focus our minds on the Spirit leads to life and peace.
—Romans 8:6 (ISV)

Affirmation/prayer: I ask your Holy Spirit to control my thoughts. This frees me of worry and indecisiveness. With your spirit, I can live a better life and be at peace.

God is my source!

June 2

FEAR—DON'T BE ITS SLAVE

For God gave us a spirit not of fear but of power and love and self-control.
—2 Timothy 1:7 (ESV)

For you did not receive the spirit of slavery to fall back into fear, but you have received the Spirit of adoption as sons, by whom we cry, "Abba! Father!"
—Romans 8:15 (ESV)

Affirmation/prayer: Fear can be a force that holds me back and keeps me from pursuing my hopes and love. This kind of fear, I know, is not from God. I will not be a slave to negative, fearful thoughts that hinder me. Lord, release me from the bondage of fear. When fear holds me back, remind me, Lord, that fear is just a feeling and not my reality. I humbly ask for the courage always to move forward in spite of my fears.

God is my source!

GIVING THANKS

Give thanks to the LORD, for he is good; his love endures forever.
—1 Chronicles 16:34 (NIV)

Affirmation/prayer: I am thankful for my life, for the chance to grow and solve problems and love and enjoy what is beautiful. I give thanks for good things and bigger visions that have come out of struggles and despair. I give thanks for family and friends. I give thanks for the peace and joy that increase daily as I follow the Lord.

God is my source!

June 4

COURAGE

Be strong and of good courage, do not fear nor be afraid of them; for the LORD your God, He is the One who goes with you. He will not leave you nor forsake you.
—Deuteronomy 31:6 (NKJV)

Yet who knows whether you have come to the kingdom for such a time as this?
—Esther 4:14 (NKJV)

Affirmation/prayer: Dear God, I need courage daily. Lord, give me courage to endure, bear up, tough it out, and keep on keeping despite my hardships and difficulties. May I remember that you are the one who keeps on walking with me. I know you will never leave me. Let your closeness light the fire of courage in me. Give me the courage and strength to be a blessing to others.

God is my source!

June 5

BEING A WINNER

Brothers and sisters, I do not consider myself yet to have taken hold of it. But one thing I do; Forgetting what is behind and straining toward what is ahead, I press on toward the goal for the prize of the upward call of God in Christ Jesus.
—Philippians 3:13–14 (NIV)

Affirmation/prayer: To win this race in life, I must set specific goals and run toward them. Living the best life this world has to offer is a good goal. Making heaven my home is an even better one. Every day I will fix my eyes on Jesus. I will not let the past spirits of fear, ego, pride, low self-esteem, or self-condemnation slow me down. I will not let other people's races distract me. Lord, strengthen my desire to run on as I deal with everyday issues. Thank you for your love and amazing grace, for they are my sources of power to run this race. Because of you, I will press on toward the goal. I won't give up, no matter what.

I am a winner!

God is my source!

June 6

GOD SAYS, "TALK TO ME"

The LORD is near to all who call on him, to all who call on him in truth.
—Psalms 145:18 (NIV)

In my distress I called to the LORD, and he answered me. From deep in the realm of the dead I called for help, and you listened to my cry.
—Jonah 2:2 (NIV)

Devote yourselves to prayer, being watchful and thankful.
—Colossians 4:2 (NIV)

Affirmation/prayer: When I have problems and feel like I don't have a friend to talk to, I will talk to God, for he is always near. I found that thankful prayers day by day breathe spiritual and emotional satisfaction I can't find anywhere else. God is my strength.

God is my source!

June 7

A GOOD DAY

May he give you the desire of your heart and make all your plans succeed.
—Psalms 20:4 (NIV)

Affirmation/prayer:
Today's plan:
1. Be at peace.
2. Remember that God is taking care of me.
3. Relax and stop trying to control all my circumstances.
4. Fall into God's strong arms with a sigh of relief.
5. Remember that no matter what my circumstances are, God's love can never be taken away from me.
6. Keep my mind and my heart on thee and not on others.
7. Be thankful always for your grace and mercy.
8. Be happy because of Your many blessings.

God is my source!

NO FEAR IN LOVE

There is no fear in love. But perfect love drives out fear, because fear has to do with punishment. The one who fears is not made perfect in love.
—1 John 4:18 (NIV)

For God has not given us a spirit of fear and timidity, but of power, love, and self-discipline.
—2 Timothy 1:7 (NIV)

Affirmation/prayer: What frightens me? When I am afraid, may I remember that I serve a God whose love covers me. God, I know you want a love that is not based on the fear of punishment or rejections. Lord, teach me how to love you and others as you would have me to love. Drive out the fear from my heart that stands in the way of healthy, peaceful relationships. As you love me, may I learn how to love others.

God loves me!

God is my source!

June 9

DAYDREAMING

Now listen, you who say, "Today or tomorrow we will go to this or that city, spend a year there, carry on business and make money." Why, you do not even know what will happen tomorrow. What is your life? You are a mist that appears for a little while and then vanishes. Instead, you ought to say, "If it is the Lord's will, we will live and do this or that."
—James 4:13–15 (NIV)

Affirmation/prayer: Your word tells me that tomorrow is not promised and I have only today. Lord, I do not know what tomorrow will bring, but you know my today and my tomorrows. Lord, I pray that I do not waste the time you have given me today with daydreams and thoughts of tomorrow. Please help me enjoy today by putting tomorrow's business in your hands. Instead of daydreaming I will work today according to your will, knowing that it is you who supplies all my needs each and every day.

God is my source!

June 10

SETTING PRIORITIES

Love the Lord your God with all your heart and with all your soul and with all your mind and with all your strength. The second is this: "Love your neighbor as yourself." There is no commandment greater than these.
—Mark 12:30–31 (NIV)

Affirmation/prayer: When I don't let loving God and myself be the top priority of my day, everything else goes awry. Loving God and myself helps me set healthy priorities. I can't love others if I don't love myself. Lord, help me to serve you and do what is best for me and others. Lord, help me prioritize my life using your love command.

God is my source!

June 11

DEPRESSION

As the deer pants for streams of water, so my soul pants for you, my God. My tears have been my food day and night, while people say to me all day long, "Where is your God?" My tears have been my meat day and night, while they continually say unto me, "Where is thy God?" Why, my soul, are you downcast? Why so disturbed within me? Put your hope in God, for I will yet praise him, my Savior and my God.
—Psalms 42:1–5 (NIV)

Affirmation/prayer: There are times when I am depressed and without hope. The magic eraser for these times is hope in God. I will praise God while counting my blessings for the good things he has already done. Lord, you have brought me through many trials. Knowing this, my hope rests on the fact that you will see me through many more. Jesus, take any depressed spirit away from me. You are my God and Savior. I will lift up my head and put my hope in You.

God is my source!

June 12

FOLLOWING GOOD ADVICE

How happy is the man who does not follow the advice of the wicked or take the path of sinners or join a group of mockers! Instead, his delight is in the LORD's instruction, and he meditates on it day and night. He is like a tree planted beside streams of water that bears its fruit in season and whose leaf does not wither. Whatever he does prospers.
—Psalms 1:1–3 (HCSB)

Affirmation/prayer: Sometimes in situations, it is difficult to know what is the right thing to do. All advice given to me is not good advice. You are my Creator, and you know the things that I need to be joyful and happy. Help me to discern what is good for me. I will listen and trust you. Thank you, God, for the strength and wisdom that comes from following your word. I will meditate on it day and night.

God is my source!

June 13

HE LOVES ME

The LORD appeared to us in the past, saying: "I have loved you with an everlasting love…"
—Jeremiah 31:3

We love because he first loved us.
—1 John 4:19 (NIV)

Affirmation/prayer: Lord, your words tells me that I am loved. When this world rejects me and tells me that I am not okay or unlovable, may I remind myself that these self-defeating words are not from you. The more I embrace your unconditional love, the more I can love myself and others.

God is my source!

June 14

GRACE

Grace to you and peace from God our Father and the Lord Jesus Christ.
—Philemon 1:3(NIV)

The grace of the Lord Jesus Christ be with your spirit.
—Philemon 1:25 (NIV)

Affirmation/prayer: Jesus, I thank you for your grace and mercy. Every time I make a good decision or avoid a pitfall, I know it is only because of your grace. Without your grace and mercy, I am nothing. With your grace and mercy, I am everything that you created me to be. Because you love, your grace and mercy will be with my spirit all of the days of my life.

God is my source!

June 15

PEACE

But the Advocate, the Holy Spirit, whom the Father will send in my name, will teach you all things and will remind you of everything I have said to you. Peace I leave with you; my peace I give you. I do not give to you as the world gives. Do not let your hearts be troubled and do not be afraid.
—John 14:26–27 (NIV)

Affirmation/prayer: Your word tells me not to let my heart be troubled, which means I have a choice. Each and every day—and many times every day—I decide whether or not be at peace. May I find peace in spite of my troubles by remembering and listening to your voice within. Lord, thank you for your gift of peace.

God is my source!

June 16

GOD'S WISDOM, NOT MINE

Thus says the Lord: "Let not the wise man boast in his wisdom, let not the mighty man boast in his might, let not the rich man boast in his riches, but let him who boasts boast in this, that he understands and knows me, that I am the Lord who practices steadfast love, justice, and righteousness in the earth. For in these things I delight, declares the Lord."
—Jeremiah 9:23–24 (ESV)

Affirmation/prayer: Am I living solely in my own wisdom and not in that of God? Do I believe God's word when it tells me that he can do for me what I cannot do for myself? Do I believe that it is God who is working things out for my good?

God is my source!

June 17

FRENEMY

If an enemy were insulting me, I could endure it; if a foe were rising against me, I could hide. But it is you, a man like myself, my companion, my close friend, with whom I once enjoyed sweet fellowship at the house of God, as we walked about among the worshipers.(NIV)

Cast your cares on the LORD and he will sustain you; he will never let the righteous be shaken.

—Psalms 55:12–14 (NIV)

Affirmation/prayer: Lord, friends and relatives will do and say things that break my heart. I ask for wisdom and peace of mind when dealing with family and friends. Help me set healthy boundaries. Jesus, when problems occur, give me the wisdom to address the issue. Your word tells me you are my support and "though I stumble, I shall not fall." Thank you for your word, which gives me strength. Your word tells me that I don't have to live life as a helpless victim. Lord, I trust in you! Thank you for being my protector and friend! Teach me how to love myself as you love me. Teach me how to love others as you would have me to love them. Most of all thank you for your gift of love.

God is my source!

June 18

GOODNESS AND MERCY

Surely goodness and mercy shall follow me all the days of my life, and I shall dwell in the house of the LORD forever.
—Psalms 23:6 (ESV)

Affirmation/prayer: As I look around me and see all of the blessings God has given me, I am assured of his undying goodness and mercy. Even when I have faced my darkest hour, God, your mercy was there beside me. When I do not feel blessed, your goodness and mercy still pursue me. Lord, I thank you for your continual goodness and mercy that will be with me here on earth and throughout eternity.

God is my source!

June 19

WELL-BALANCED DIET

How blessed is the person, who does not take the advice of the wicked, who does not stand on the path with sinners, and who does not sit in the seat of mockers. But he delights in the LORD's instruction, and meditates in his instruction day and night. He will be like a tree planted by streams of water, yielding its fruit in its season, and whose leaf does not wither. He will prosper in everything he does.
—Psalms 1:1–3 (ISV)

But he answered, "It is written, 'One must not live on bread alone, but on every word coming out of the mouth of God.'"
—Matthew 4:4 (ISV)

Affirmation/prayer: When I feed only the physical and intellectual part of me, the soul and sprit become weak and undernourished. This results in feelings of depression, defeatism, loneliness, hopelessness, fear, and so forth. Jesus, please help me to put away ego and intellectual pride as I give way to meditating on your words. Holy Spirit, fill me with the nourishment of your word. Show me the path to a well-balanced diet of the word so I may feed my body, my spirit, and my soul.

God is my source!

June 20

GENTLE WHISPER

The LORD said, "Go out and stand on the mountain in the presence of the LORD, for the LORD is about to pass by." Then a great and powerful wind tore the mountains apart and shattered the rocks before the LORD, but the LORD was not in the wind. After the wind there was an earthquake, but the LORD was not in the earthquake. After the earthquake came a fire, but the LORD was not in the fire. And after the fire came a gentle whisper. When Elijah heard it, he pulled his cloak over his face and went out and stood at the mouth of the cave. Then a voice said to him, "What are you doing here, Elijah?"
—1 Kings 19:11–13 (NIV)

Affirmation/prayer: Your word teaches me that the voice of God is often that still, small inner voice that I call instinct or intuition. Lord, quiet my spirit so that I may hear you above all the activities and noises of this world. During meditation and prayer, may I hear your voice speaking to me, leading and guiding me forward in the direction you would have me to go. Amen.

God is my source!

June 21

NO MORE EXCUSES

I prayed to the Lord, and I praised him. If my thoughts had been sinful, he would have refused to hear me. But God did listen and answered my prayer.
—Psalms 66:17–19

What should we say? Should we keep on sinning, so that God's gift of undeserved grace will show up even better? No, we should not! If we are dead to sin, how can we go on sinning?
—Romans 6:1–2 (CEV)

Affirmation/prayer: No more excuses: a) the devil made me do it; b) it is because of what they did (parents, friends, coworkers, etc.); c) I didn't know any better; d) next time I will do better; e) it is a little white sin. The truth is, Lord, that most of the sin in my heart is because I love the sin and its benefits in this world. May I take an honest look at my thoughts and actions so that I may love you more than the things I do against your will? It is me, Lord, standing in the need of prayer. May your love and grace abound, Lord Jesus, as I live as you would have me to live—with no more excuses!

God is my source!

June 22

HERE AM I, LORD; SEND ME

Then I heard the voice of the Lord saying, "Whom shall I send? And who will go for us?" And I said, "Here am I. Send me!"
—Isaiah 6:8 (NIV)

Never be lacking in zeal, but keep your spiritual fervor, serving the Lord. Be joyful in hope, patient in affliction, faithful in prayer. Share with the Lord's people who are in need. Practice hospitality.
—Romans 12:11–13 (NIV)

Affirmation/prayer: Lord, you have been so good to me. Your word tells me to be zealous as I serve you. I will not hit the mute button but will be attentive to find ways in which you would have me serve others. Fill me with hope, patience, and love so that I may pass these on to others. I pray for the obedience that when I see the need, I can say, "Here I am, Lord; send me."

God is my source!

June 23

GOD'S ABOUNDING LOVE

You, Lord, are forgiving and good, abounding in love to all who call to you.
—Psalms 86:5 (NIV)

Give thanks to the Lord, for he is good; his love endures forever.
—1 Chronicles 16:34 (NIV)

Affirmation/prayer: I shall think of your love daily and your awesomeness so that I may remember the God I serve. In you there is joy, peace, happiness, and love.

God is my source!

June 24

I AM NAKED

For the word of God is alive and active. Sharper than any double-edged sword, it penetrates even to dividing soul and spirit, joints and marrow; it judges the thoughts and attitudes of the heart. Nothing in all creation is hidden from God's sight. Everything is uncovered and laid bare before the eyes of him to whom we must give account. Therefore, since we have a great high priest who has ascended into heaven, Jesus the Son of God, let us hold firmly to the faith we profess.

—Hebrews 4:12–14 (NIV)

Affirmation/prayer: Jesus, I am naked before you. You see my mind, spirit, body, and soul. You know my affections, thoughts, and motives behind everything that I do. You are acquainted with all of my sorrows. Lord Jesus, I confess my sins only so that you know that I am aware of them. Give me the strength to hold on to the faith so that I may not sin against you. As you judge my thoughts and attitudes, I ask that you forgive me when I do wrong. Jesus, please hold my hand and keep it, for I am naked until you come again.

God is my source!

June 25

MERCY AND FORGIVENESS

Don't tear your clothing in your grief, but tear your hearts instead. Return to the LORD your God, for he is merciful and compassionate, slow to get angry and filled with unfailing love. He is eager to relent and not punish.
—Joel 2:13 (NIV)

You, Lord, are forgiving and good, abounding in love to all who call to you.
—Psalms 86:5 (NIV)

Affirmation/prayer: No longer will I hide or leave God because of my mistakes. The belief that you are a God who is eager to condemn me is a lie of Satan. Even on my worst days, you, Lord, are just waiting for me to acknowledge and repent of my mistakes. Your love will never fail me. There is no sin that your love cannot cover when I turn to you for forgiveness. Lord, please forgive me of any wrong that I have done to you or others. Thank you for love, grace, and mercy.

God is my source!

June 26

LOVE

For God so loved the world, that he gave his only Son, that whoever believes in him should not perish but have eternal life.
—John 3:16 (NIV)

Affirmation/prayer: Teach me your love, dear God. Teach me how to love as you love. Teach me how to accept and love myself. Teach me how to love others and share your kindness and mercy. Help me teach others of a God who loved the world so much that he gave his only son for our sins so that all may have eternal life. Most of all thank you for a love that sets me free.

God is my source!

June 27

WRONGDOERS

But if you do what is wrong, you will be paid back for the wrong you have done. For God has no favorites.
—Colossians 3:25

Affirmation/prayer: May I remember that I work for you, Lord. May I not treat others wrongly. When others do me wrong (and in this evil world, it will happen), may I remember the wrongdoer will be paid back without exception. Help me put my trust in you. Keep me from the evil one. Help me to set healthy boundaries of protection in all my relationships. Thank you in advance for a beautiful and prosperous day.

God is my source!

June 28

SHINING LIKE A STAR

Do everything without grumbling or arguing, so that you may become blameless and pure, "children of God without fault in a warped and crooked generation [society]." Then you will shine among them like stars in the sky.
—Philippians 2:14–15 (NIV)

Affirmation/prayer: It is so easy to find fault and grumble about the way things are in society. Sometimes I may find myself in the presence of unforgiving people on the streets, at work, and even at home. Lord, let your spirit be my director and not my ego when dealing with others. Please let my speech and actions be the shining light of yours for others.

God is my source!

June 29

MY WORDS

Don't use foul or abusive language. Let everything you say be good and helpful, so that your words will be an encouragement to those who hear them.
—Ephesians 4:29 (NLT)

Affirmation/prayer: Lord, help me to guard my tongue, no matter what situation I find myself in. When I speak, may it be an encouragement to others.

God is my source!

June 30

THIS DAY

This is the day the LORD has made. We will rejoice and be glad in it.
—Psalms 118:24 (NLT)

Affirmation/prayer: Every day I wake up, I will thank God for another day. I realize that I do not have the power to control every situation that comes my way today. I can, however, control how I think. Therefore, I will look for all the good things this day has to offer. I will find joy knowing that God is in control.

God is my source!

July

ALPHA AND OMEGA

I am Alpha and Omega, the beginning and the end, the first and the last.
—Revelation 22:13 (KJV)

Affirmation/prayer: Wherever I have gone, he has gone before me. Wherever I shall go, He will go before me.

God is my source!

July 2

POWER WITHIN

Now to him who is able to do immeasurably more than all we ask or imagine, according to his power that is at work within us.
—Ephesians 3:20 (NIV)

Children, you belong to God, and you have defeated these enemies. God's Spirit is in you and is more powerful than the one who is in the world.
—1 John 4:4(CEV)

Affirmation/prayer: As a child of God, I have the power within me to move past the pain and disappointments of life. When I say, "I can't go on, Lord," open my eyes that I may see and understand your power within me. Show me how to move past my weaknesses and disappointments. Show me when and how to just move on in your strength.

God is my source!

July 3

GOD IS FAITHFUL

Let's do our best to know the LORD. His coming is as certain as the morning sun; he will refresh us like rain renewing the earth in the springtime.
—Hosea 6:3 (CEV)

Affirmation/prayer: How beautiful are your words. They teach me you are as faithful as the seasons of the year.

God is my source!

July 4

HUMBLENESS OR HUMILIATION

Humble yourselves, therefore, under God's mighty hand, that he may lift you up in due time, casting all your anxiety on Him, because He cares for you.
—1 Peter 5:6–7

The pride of your heart has deceived you…
—Obadiah 1:3 (NIV)

Affirmation/prayer: It is better to humble myself under the will of God than be humiliated by mankind. I am only humiliated when my ego attaches itself to the negative opinions of others. Therefore, I will drop pride and ego and humbly submit my image of self into the mighty hands of God, who cares for me. In him I will boast. It is God who lifts me up in due time.

God is my source!

July 5

TEACH THE CHILDREN

Love the LORD your God with all your heart, with all your soul, and with all your strength. These commandments that I give you today are to be on your hearts. Impress them on your children. Talk about them when you sit at home and when you walk along the road, when you lie down and when you get up.
—Deuteronomy 6:5–7 (NIV)

Affirmation/prayer: Every day is a good day to teach the children how to grow spiritually and emotionally. They are never too young or old to learn about Jesus. May I teach them how to "love the Lord with all their heart, with all their soul, and with all their strength." May my life be a witness to the children that this is possible. Thank you, Lord, for the little children in my life.

God is my source!

July 6

IF ONLY I HAD KNOWN

For the LORD grants wisdom! From his mouth come knowledge and understanding. He grants a treasure of common sense to the honest. He is a shield to those who walk with integrity. He guards the paths of the just and protects those who are faithful to him. Then you will understand what is right, just, and fair, and you will find the right way to go.
—Proverbs 2:6–9 (NLT)

Affirmation/prayer: God's wisdom keeps me from making wrong decisions, thus preventing me from saying, "If only I had known." Remove guilt, Lord; give me insight to make my past failures my wisdom. Surround me with the wise counsel of those who have my best interests at heart. Give me wisdom, patience, and courage as I go through the challenges of life. May I seek and follow your lead as I make all decisions. Lord, show me the right way to go (succeed).

God, you are my source!

UNDERSTANDING

Wisdom is the principal thing; therefore, get wisdom: and with all thy getting get understanding.
—Proverbs 4:7 (NKJV)

In his heart a man plans his course but the Lord determines his steps.
—Proverbs 16:9 (KJV)

Affirmation/prayer: I know that in order to gain more understanding, I must first act on the knowledge that comes from above. My intellectual awareness alone is not enough, considering that it is God who controls my destiny. In my affairs today, Lord, increase my awareness of you. I pray for your wisdom and understanding in making all my decisions.

God is my source!

July 8

DEALING WITH OFFENSES

Be angry and do not sin. Don't let the sun go down on your anger, nor give place to the devil.
—Ephesians 4:26–27 (NKJV)

Let all bitterness, wrath, anger, clamor, and evil speaking be put away from you, with all malice. And be kind to one another, tenderhearted, forgiving one another, even as God in Christ forgave you.
—Ephesians 4:31–32 (NKJV)

Affirmation/prayer: Lord help me to not get angry easily or be offended for no reason at all. Where others have offended me, give me the wisdom and courage to speak my truth in love. May I hate the fault and not the person who has offended me. When I am angry because of a fault within, I don't want to take it out on those around me. Please help me to forgive others quickly and not hold onto grudges. Help me always be forgiving and tenderhearted to all, to everyone I encounter, just as you are to me.

God is my source!

July 9

THE HOLY SPIRIT, MY INTERCESSOR

In the same way, the Spirit helps us in our weakness. We do not know what we ought to pray for, but the Spirit himself intercedes for us through wordless groans. And he who searches our hearts knows the mind of the Spirit, because the Spirit intercedes for God's people in accordance with the will of God. And we know that in all things God works for the good of those who love him, who have been called according to his purpose.
—Romans 8:26–28 (NIV)

Affirmation/prayer: God, spirit is the power through which I am able to become all that God intends me to be. It is the spirit that helps me when I am weak and confused. When I come to the end of my hopes, abilities, and dreams, the spirit searches my heart and leads me on in God's footsteps. God's spirit within gives me hope and faith, which flows into all areas of my life. With faith and hope, I can do that which once I thought was impossible.

God is my source!

July 10

A FRIEND

I look for someone to come and help me, but no one gives me a passing thought! No one will help me; no one cares a bit what happens to me. Then I pray to you, O LORD. I say, "You are my place of refuge. You are all I really want in life."
—Psalms 142:4–5 (NLT)

Jesus understands every weakness of ours, because he was tempted in every way that we are. But he did not sin!
—Hebrews 4:15

Affirmation/prayer: There will be times when not even my friends understand how I feel. When it seems that I have no one to care or have my back, it is good to know that my true friend is always just a prayer away. Jesus you are my true friend. Hebrews 4:15 tells me you listen, empathize, and have been tempted in every way yet you did not give in. Your word speaks that in You I have a friend that I can find a safe place to land. Your love never fails.

God is my source!

July 11

MY HELP

Our help comes from the LORD, who made heaven and earth.
—Psalms 124:8 (GNT)

Affirmation/prayer: Just knowing that I have help from God helps me face whatever today brings, including my giants.

God is my source!

July 12

A NEW DAY

The faithful love of the LORD never ends! His mercies never cease. Great is his faithfulness; his mercies begin afresh each morning.
—Lamentations 3:22–23 (NLT)

Affirmation/prayer: Yesterday is gone. I can't go back in time and undo my mistakes and failures. I thank God that each morning he gives me new mercies love, hope, and a new way to live. Lord, you have been good to me in the past. Thank you, God, for another day and all its blessings. Thank you for your mercy and grace.

God is my source!

July 13

STRENGTH FOR TODAY

You are my strength, I sing praise to you; you, God, are my fortress, my God on whom I can rely.
—Psalms 59:17 (NIV)

Affirmation/prayer: Where I am weak, he is strong! I do not have sufficient strength to face today alone. Thank you, God, for being a fortress daily that keeps me when my enemies attack. When I am weak, your strength keeps me calm inside, both emotionally and spiritually.

God is my source!

July 14

WEALTH AND MONEY

"The silver is mine and the gold is mine," declares the LORD Almighty.
—Haggai 2:8(NIV)

Command those who are rich in this present world not to be arrogant nor to put their hope in wealth, which is so uncertain, but to put their hope in God, who richly provides us with everything for our enjoyment. Command them to do good, to be rich in good deeds, and to be generous and willing to share. In this way they will lay up treasure for themselves as a firm foundation for the coming age, so that they may take hold of the life that is truly life.
—1 Timothy 6:17–19(NIV)

For where your treasure is, there your heart will be also.
—Matthew 6:21 (NIV)

Affirmation/prayer: Thank you, God, for all that I own. No matter if I am wealthy or poor, I still need you, Lord, to supply all my needs. I ask for divine wisdom when taking an honest look at my finances. Show me when and how to share my possessions with those whom you would have me help. My blessings and hope are because of God.

God is my source!

July 15

FEAR

For God has not given us a spirit of fear and timidity, but of power, love, and self-discipline.
—2 Timothy 1:7(NLT)

Don't be afraid, for I am with you. Don't be discouraged, for I am your God. I will strengthen you and help you. I will hold you up with my victorious right hand.
—Isaiah 41:10 (NLT)

Affirmation/prayer: My fears can be real or imagined. If I don't examine my fears and give them to God, I will never fulfill my purpose for living. God, your word says that the spirit of fear is not from you. I don't want to live a fearful life. Therefore I pray for your strength and wisdom to move beyond all fears that hinder me. I pray that you give me courage to remove my fears and replace them with your spirit of power, love, and self-discipline.

God is my source!

RIVERS WITHIN

Whoever believes in me, as Scripture has said, rivers of living water will flow from within them.
—John 7:38(NIV)

I pray that God, the source of hope, will fill you completely with joy and peace because you trust in him. Then you will overflow with confident hope through the power of the Holy Spirit.
—Romans 15:13 (NIV)

Affirmation/prayer: As a Christian, the Holy Spirit is inside of me like rivers of living water. Like rivers that constantly flow, I am filled daily with faith courage and hope. When I am thirsty, I will take a drink from within and let the Holy Spirit quench my thirst with love, joy, peace, patience, kindness, goodness, faithfulness, gentleness, and self-control. Thank you, Jesus, for your Holy Spirit that lives within like rivers of living water that, never dries up.

God is my source!

July 17

SELF-AWARENESS 2

We may think we know what is right, but the LORD is the judge of our motives.
—Proverbs 16:2(CEV)

But you want complete honesty, so teach me true wisdom.
—Psalms 51:6 (CEV)

Affirmation/prayer: Grant me the ability to look within me with rigorous honesty. May I examine my heart in all areas of my life. Where I find things within that I need to change, give me the strength to make a change. Let me not listen to the voice of the accuser and blame others for my faults. You desire truth within, so I ask that you strengthen me so that I may take a good look at the motives for doing the things I do. Help me remove and not ignore anything that does not line up with your truth. Lord, help me see myself as you see me. Please give me your wisdom, love me, and strengthen me as I become whole.

God is my source!

July 18

MY SHEPHERD

The LORD is my shepherd; I shall not want. He makes me lie down in green pastures. He leads me beside still waters. He restores my soul. He leads me in paths of righteousness for his name's sake. Yea, though I walk through the valley of the shadow of death, I will fear no evil; For You are with me; Your rod and Your staff, they comfort me.
—Psalms 23:1–4 (NKJV)

Affirmation/prayer: Like a shepherd, God and his word lead me, instruct me, and comfort me. When I feel lost and afraid, it is because I am not close enough to the shepherd. Lord, help me stay close to thee.

God is my source!

July 19

STRENGTH IN STRENGTHENING

But I begged for you, that your faith may not fail. And you, when you have turned back, strengthen your brothers.
—Luke 22:32 (HCSB)

That is, that I may be comforted together with you by the mutual faith both of you and me.
—Romans 1:12 (KJV)

Affirmation/prayer: I will use all my abilities and God's spiritual gifts to soothe, console, and uplift my friends. By doing so, my friends, family, and those around me are strengthened, and so am I. Lord, let my spiritual gifts be of service to you and others.

God is my source!

July 20

WILL TRUST IN YOU

Those who know your name trust in you, for you, LORD, have never forsaken those who seek you.

—Psalms 9:10 (NIV)

But I trust in you, LORD; I say, "You are my God."
—Psalms 31:14 (NIV)

Affirmation/prayer: To say "I trust God" is quick and easy. Learning to put my trust in God grows stronger and deeper each day that I rely on him during my bad times and my good times. Like taking the first step on a long journey, each day may I say, "You are my God. I will trust in you."

God is my source!

July 21

MY BURDEN BEARER

Praise be to the Lord, to God our Savior, who daily bears our burdens.
—Psalms 68:19 (NIV)

Cast all your anxiety on him because he cares for you.
—1 Peter 5:7 (NIV)

I can do all this through him who gives me strength.
—Philippians 4:13 (NIV)

Affirmation/prayer: Stress and anxiety comes in when I let my ego tell me that I have superpowers and can get everything done in one day. As I drop my ego and self-will, God releases my stress and anxiety by showing me how to accomplish one thing at a time in one day at a time.

God is my source!

July 22

ENCOURAGEMENT

But encourage one another daily, as long as it is called "Today," so that none of you may be hardened by sin's deceitfulness.
—Hebrews 3:13 (NIV)

Affirmation/prayer: I don't live in this world alone. It is the very encouragement of others that help keeps me from the sins that I struggle with. God, may I be an encouragement to someone caught up in their own personal struggles to return to you.

God is my source!

July 23

REFRESHED

The Sovereign LORD has given me his words of wisdom, so that I know how to comfort the weary. Morning by morning he wakens me and opens my understanding to his will. The Sovereign LORD has spoken to me, and I have listened. I have not rebelled or turned away.
—Isaiah 50:4–5 (NLT)

Affirmation/prayer: Each and every morning, the Lord refreshes me with his grace, love, joy, and peace. May I learn from him as a student so that I may minister to those without hope.

God is my source!

July 24

WORD POWER

The tongue can bring death or life; those who love to talk will reap the consequences.
—Proverbs 18:21 (NLT)

Affirmation/prayer: Truly, I will eat the fruit of the words I speak to others and myself. Teach me how to speak positive words to others and myself at all times. Today I will bring life to myself by reaping the fruit of the many positive words that I speak to me.

Positive words:

Today is a good day.
God loves me.
It will be a peaceful day because God's peace surrounds me.
God and I am enough.
God will supply all my needs.
I am a beautiful, wonderful person full of peace, joy, and love.
I can succeed!
I will succeed!
God is my source!
End of story!

July 25

DOORS

When one door of happiness closes, another opens; but often we look so long at the closed door that we do not see the one which has been opened for us.
—Helen Keller

Ask and it will be given to you; seek and you will find; knock and the door will be opened to you.
—Matthew 7:7

Affirmation/prayer: Today, may I not live this day in thoughts about the "good old days." May I not live today in past regrets. Instead, Lord, open my eyes to the good things today brings. May I move forward as I open doors of new friendships, opportunities, and blessings.

God is my source!

July 26

FEARS

*The LORD is my light and my salvation; whom shall I fear? the
LORD is the strength of my life; of whom shall I be afraid?*
—Psalms 27:1 (NKJV)

Affirmation/prayer: I will face my fears head-on, knowing
that God is in charge. He is my light and my strength. He is
not very far away.

God is my source!

July 27

SOUL AND BODY

When I kept silent, my bones wasted away through my groaning all day long.
—Psalms 32:3(NIV)

Then I acknowledged my sin to you and did not cover up my iniquity. I said, "I will confess my transgressions to the LORD." And you forgave the guilt of my sin. Therefore let all the faithful pray to you while you may be found; surely the rising of the mighty waters will not reach them. You are my hiding place! You protect me from trouble, and you put songs in my heart because you have saved me.
—Psalms 32:5–7 (NIV)

Affirmation/prayer: Your word tells me there is a relationship with my inner soul and my outer body. Lord, I give you my sins and the pain within. I will not try to drown out my feelings with anything. The confession of my sins is the only way that I can get relief from the things that overcome me. Lord, please forgive my sins and heal my mind, body, and soul. Put your joy and a new song in my heart.

God is my source!

July 28

DAILY BLESSINGS

Because of the LORD's great love we are not consumed, for his compassions never fail. They are new every morning; great is your faithfulness. I say to myself, "The LORD is my portion; therefore I will wait for him." The LORD is good to those whose hope is in him, to the one who seeks him.
—Lamentations 3:22–25 (NIV)

Affirmation/prayer: Every morning God has just what I need to face another day. Every morning God has new blessings for me to receive them. Every morning I can count on God to be faithful. Every morning I can expect to receive God's mercy, compassion, and grace. Every morning and all day, I will trust and wait on God.

Thank you, Lord, for a new day!

God is my source!

July 29

ROCK OF PERFECT PEACE

You will keep in perfect peace all who trust in you, all whose thoughts are fixed on you! Trust in the LORD forever, for the LORD, the LORD himself, is the Rock eternal.
—Isaiah 26:3–4 (NLT)

Affirmation/prayer: I find myself on unstable ground when I seek peace in people, possessions, human philosophies, and my own will. Lord, your word promises me an eternal peace that comes when my thoughts are fixed on you. Lord, guide my thoughts into your perfect peace. Help me stand on the rock of perfect peace that you have provided for me.

God is my source!

July 30

NEVER STOP PRAYING

Certain thoughts are prayers. There are moments when, whatever be the attitude of the body, the soul is on its knees.
—Victor Hugo

Always be joyful. Never stop praying.
—1 Thessalonians 5:16–17 (NLT)

Affirmation/prayer: There will never come a time that I will not need to pray. Prayer is such a powerful tool that I have at my disposal to communicate with God. I am wise when I carry prayer with me throughout the day. I will use prayer in the morning to prepare me for the day. I will use prayer to guard my tongue when responding to others. When in doubt of how to respond to others, I will use prayer to lead me and guide me. I will use prayer all day to thank God that I am his child.

God is my source!

July 31

HER STRENGTH

She is clothed with strength and honor, and she can laugh at the time to come.
—Proverbs 31:25

Affirmation/prayer: I have been through some rough times in my life. Through it all, I've learn to trust in Jesus; I've learned to trust in God.

God is my source and my strength!

August

August 1

HOPE NOT SHAME

We can rejoice, too, when we run into problems and trials, for we know that they help us develop endurance. And endurance develops strength of character, and character strengthens our confident hope of salvation. And this hope will not lead to disappointment. For we know how dearly God loves us, because he has given us the Holy Spirit to fill our hearts with his love.
—Romans 5:3–5 (NLT)

Affirmation/prayer: No matter what the circumstances that I am going through, I always have hope in the love of God. Because of his love, there is no shame when I encounter failures and trials. Shame will not defeat me when I put my hope in his love that never fails. I may not understand why problems arise, but I know that God still loves me. Lord, let me feel your Holy Spirit within so that I will never be defeated by my mistakes or the trouble that seems to come out of nowhere. May your love and the Holy Spirit within help me grow in patience that produces character, which produces hope.

God is my source!

August 2

WHAT MATTERS MOST

All those the Father gives me will come to me, and whoever comes to me I will never drive away.
—John 6:37(NIV)

Affirmation/prayer: Jesus, I come to you in prayer knowing you will not turn me away. It doesn't matter who I was or who I am now; my life matters because I am yours.

When I pray to you, and the pains of life remain, it does not mean you have not heard me. By faith I willingly place myself under your control, safety, and protection. Thank you for answering all my prayers.

Jesus, you matter most! You give me good things.

You are my source!

August 3

JOYFULLY LEAD

You make known to me the path of life; you will fill me with joy in your presence, with eternal pleasures at your right hand.
—Psalms 16:11 (NIV)

Affirmation/prayer: Lord, thank you for being by my side, leading and guiding me. You are with me not because I deserve it, but because you love me. Joyful and happy am I when I follow your lead.

God is my source!

August 4

IN HIM WE LIVE

God did this so that they would seek him and perhaps reach out for him and find him, though he is not far from any one of us. For in him we live and move and have our being. As some of your own poets have said, "We are his offspring."
—Acts 17:27–28 (NIV)

Affirmation/prayer: Lord, everything I am and everything I will be is because of you. May I not forget this as I face today's challenges. Help me stop, get out of my own head and strength, and seek your power. It is by your strength I will succeed. In you I will live!

God is my source!

August 5

MY TRUE SELF

And be renewed in the spirit of your mind; And that ye put on the new man, which after God is created in righteousness and true holiness.
—Ephesians 4:23–24 (KJV)

Affirmation/prayer: Lord, you created me, and that says I am good. Lord, I humbly open my heart to you giving to you my faults and all my assets.

Take away the person that this world says I am. Restore in me a heart created by you. Only then can I see in me the wonderful creation of God. This is good. This is my true self.

God is my source!

August 6

BEAUTY OF NOT KNOWING

Even though the fig trees have no blossoms, and there are no grapes on the vines; even though the olive crop fails, and the fields lie empty and barren; even though the flocks die in the fields, and the cattle barns are empty, yet I will rejoice in the LORD! I will be joyful in the God of my salvation!
—Habakkuk 3:17–18

And God will generously provide all you need. Then you will always have everything you need and plenty left over to share with others.
—2 Corinthians 9:8 (NLT)

Affirmation/Prayer: The beauty of faith is seen in my uncertain times. I say to myself, "I don't know if he will or won't, but I do know this one thing: my God is able!"

God is my source!

August 7

MY CONFIDENT HOPE

So be strong and courageous, all you who put your hope in the LORD.
—Psalms 31:24

We were given this hope when we were saved. (If we already have something, we don't need to hope for it.) But if we look forward to something we don't yet have, we must wait patiently and confidently.
—Romans 8:24–25 (NLT)

Affirmation/prayer: You have been with me in the past, and I have confident hope that you are walking with me now. Today I will have courage and strength because I have confident hope in you. When I am tempted to give in to stressful situations, it is hope that will bring me your peace. Thank you that I need not know what tomorrow will bring because I can put my confident hope in you.

God is my source!

August 8

HAVING A GOOD SELF-IMAGE

You made all the delicate, inner parts of my body and knit me together in my mother's womb. Thank you for making me so wonderfully complex! Your workmanship is marvelous—how well I know it.
—Psalms 139:13–14 (NLT)

By his divine power, God has given us everything we need for living a godly life. We have received all of this by coming to know him, the one who called us to himself by means of his marvelous glory and excellence.
—2 Peter 1:3 (NLT)

Affirmation/prayer: Having a good self-image means starting each day remembering that I am God's creation and he has made me in his image. Having a good self-image means remembering that I am uniquely and wonderfully made. Having a good self-image comes from remembering that inside of me is everything that I need to succeed in this world through Jesus. Having a good self-image means that I take the time to be thankful for the small and big things that I can do daily. Thank you, Lord, for making me. God is my source!

August 9

UNDERSTANDING GOD

In the beginning the Word already existed. The Word was with God, and the Word was God. He existed in the beginning with God. God created everything through him, and nothing was created except through him. The Word gave life to everything that was created, and his life brought light to everyone.
—John 1:1–4 (NLT)

Affirmation/prayer: Jesus, your word speaks to me of who you are. If I don't read it, you become a God of what I am told. In your words is life. Speak to my heart through your words so I can learn of a God that loves me more than I could ever understand.

God is my source!

August 10

TODAY IS A GOOD DAY

*Let your hope keep you joyful, be patient in your troubles, and
pray at all times.*
—Romans 12:12 (GNT)

Affirmation/prayer: It's gonna be a good day! A good day
means living in hope, not despair. A good day means living today in patience when trouble finds me, knowing that even this
shall pass. A good day is when I invite God into my day all day
long through prayer. Again, I say, "It's gonna be a good day."

God is my source!

August 11

CHERISH EACH MOMENT

There is a time for everything, and a season for every activity under the heavens.
—Ecclesiastes 3:1 (NIV)

Affirmation/prayer:

I will ask God when to begin a thing.

I will ask God when to finish a thing.

I will ask when to be at peace as I work through each thing.

I will ask God to let go of the need to be in control.

I will ask God to remind me that all thing will work out in its own time.

I will ask God to help me cherish each moment.

God is my source!

August 12

KEEP ON KEEPING ON

Therefore we do not give up. Even though our outer person is being destroyed, our inner person is being renewed day by day.
—2 Corinthians 4:16 (HCSB)

Affirmation/prayer: Lord, may I remember that changes do not always happen quickly. Help me realize that good things often happen slowly and one day at a time. Lord, help me to keep on keeping on as you change my circumstances. Lord, thank you for renewing the inner me day by day.

God is my source!

August 13

FORGIVEN

For everyone has sinned; we all fall short of God's glorious standard. Yet God, in his grace, freely makes us right in his sight. He did this through Christ Jesus when he freed us from the penalty for our sins.
—Romans 3:23–24 (NLT)

Yes, what joy for those whose record the LORD has cleared of sin.
—Romans 4:8 (NLT)

Affirmation/prayer: Jesus, as your child, I freely give you the sins in my life. Free me of the guilt and shame that I feel because of my past. Restore in me a clean heart so that I may serve you.

God is my source!

August 14

WORRYING

Can all your worries add a single moment to your life?
—Luke 12:25(NLT)

Give all your worries and cares to God, for he cares about you.
—1 Peter 5:7 (NLT)

Always be joyful. Never stop praying. Be thankful in all circumstances, for this is God's will for you who belong to Christ Jesus.
—1 Thessalonians 5:16–18 (NLT)

Affirmation/prayer: I will face my obstacles with prayer and thanksgiving. Lord, give me your grace not to worry about anything. Give me your joy. Lord, your will, not my will.

God is my source!

August 15

IT IS WELL WITH MY SOUL

God is our refuge and strength, always ready to help in times of trouble. So we will not fear when earthquakes come and the mountains crumble into the sea. Let the oceans roar and foam. Let the mountains tremble as the waters surge!

The LORD of Heaven's Armies is here among us…
—Psalms 46:1–3, 11 (NLT)

And I will ask the Father, and he will give you another Advocate, who will never leave you.
—John 14:16 (NLT)

Affirmation/prayer: No matter what the situation outside of me, I have peace because of the God who lives inside of me. He is my help in times of trouble. It is well with my soul.

God is my source!

August 16

TROUBLE DOESN'T LAST ALWAYS

Sing praise to the LORD, you His godly ones, And give thanks to His holy name. For His anger is but for a moment, His favor is for a lifetime; Weeping may last for the night, But a shout of joy comes in the morning.
—Psalms 30:4–5 (NLT)

Affirmation/prayer: Lord Jesus, when I cry at night, you see my tears. In spite of my mistakes, you are a loving and forgiving God. Trouble doesn't last always because when it is all said and done, you are my strength.

God is my source!

August 17

I WON'T GIVE UP

I had fainted, unless I had believed to see the goodness of the LORD in the land of the living. Wait on the LORD: be of good courage, and he shall strengthen thine heart: wait, I say, on the LORD.
—Psalms 27:13–14 (KJV)

Affirmation/prayer: I have seen you do good things for me in the past. Therefore I won't give in. I won't give up. Seeing all he has done for me gives me strength courage and hope. Surely I will see many more blessings in the future. I will wait on the Lord.

God is my source!

August 18

HEALTHY, WEALTHY, AND WISE

Healthy

Don't ever think that you are wise enough, but respect the LORD and stay away from evil. This will make you healthy, and you will feel strong.

—Proverbs 3:7–8 (CEV)

Wealthy

Honor the LORD by giving him your money and the first part of all your crops. Then you will have more grain and grapes (wealth) than you will ever need.

—Proverbs 3:9–10 (CEV)

Wise

With all your heart you must trust the LORD and not your own judgment. Always let him lead you, and he will clear the road for you to follow.

—Proverbs 3: (CEV)

Affirmation/prayer: I will put my trust in the Lord. All I need to succeed is found in Him.

God is my source!

August 19

GET A GOOD UNDERSTANDING

Get wisdom, get understanding; do not forget my words or turn away from them. Do not forsake wisdom, and she will protect you; love her, and she will watch over you. The beginning of wisdom is this: Get wisdom. Though it cost all you have, get understanding.
—Proverbs 4:5–7 (NIV)

Affirmation/prayer: Lord, before I speak or do anything today, help me to get a good understanding. Amen.

God is my source!

August 20

BE YE HOLY

So you must live as God's obedient children. Don't slip back into your old ways of living to satisfy your own desires. You didn't know any better than. Always live as God's holy people should, because God is the one who chose you, and he is holy.
—1 Peter 1:14–15 (NLT)

Affirmation/prayer: Lord, what I do and say speaks volumes as to who I am. My family, friends, and fellow coworkers all know me by my conversations and my actions. I want to consistently live a life according to your will. A life that shows how much you love me. Lord, you are holy, loving, and kind to me. Please help me be holy, loving, and kind to others.

God is my source!

August 21

COMPULSIVE BEHAVIORS

For the world offers only a craving for physical pleasure, a craving for everything we see, and pride in our achievements and possessions. These are not from the Father, but are from this world. And this world is fading away, along with everything that people crave. But anyone who does what pleases God will live forever.
—1 John 2:16–17 (NLT)

You will show me the way of life, granting me the joy of your presence and the pleasures of living with you forever.
—Psalms 16:11(NLT)

Affirmation/prayer: I will not give into my compulsive and out-of-control behaviors. Out-of-control spending, eating, talking without thinking first, anger, and jealousy are all signs that my self-will is running the show. I will surrender my will to God's will by following his path. Only in God's will I experience the fullness of true pleasures, happiness, and joy, and with them, peace.

God is my source!

August 22

TAKE HEART AND WAIT

Do not let your hearts be troubled. You believe in God; believe also in me.
—John 14:1 (NIV)

Wait for the LORD; be strong and take heart and wait for the LORD.
—Psalms 27:14 (NIV)

Affirmation/prayer: Everything works out in its own due time. Lord, help me trust and wait on you.

God is my source!

August 23

HOW TO KEEP A COOL HEAD

My dear brothers and sisters, understand this: Everyone should be quick to listen, slow to speak, and slow to anger.
—James 1:19 (CSB)

A man of knowledge restrains his words, and a man of understanding keeps a cool head.
—Proverbs 17:27 (CSB)

Affirmation/prayer: Lord, help me not rely on my negative ego and self-centered pride to dictate how I react to circumstances outside of myself. Instead of reacting in fear, jealousy, pride, or anger, Lord, please show me how to use my God-given wisdom when listening and reacting to others. Disagreements will happen in life. Give me the wisdom and knowledge to listen, keep calm, speak my truth in love, and not be so quick to become angry. Help me, Lord, keep a cool head.

God is my source!

August 24

GENTLENESS

Let your gentleness be evident to all. The Lord is near.
—Philippians 4:5 (NIV)

A gentle answer turns away wrath, but a harsh word stirs up anger.
—Proverbs 15:1 (NIV)

Let your conversation be always full of grace, seasoned with salt, so that you may know how to answer everyone.
—Colossians 4:6 (NIV)

Affirmation/prayer: Lord, your word tells me that a gentle spirit is a valuable asset living in today's world. In my busy, overactive schedule, Lord, please help me to slow down and be gentle in my dealings with everyone, especially those who are angry. As I discipline my children, help me be gentle so that their self-esteem is not damaged because of my harsh words. When my friends and family are hurting, give me your gentle spirit so that I may be of comfort to them. Thank you for the love and gentleness you have shown me.

God is my source!

August 25

BELIEF

"If you can?" said Jesus. "Everything is possible for one who believes." "I do believe; help me overcome my unbelief!"
—Mark 9:23–24 (NIV)

I am the resurrection and the life. The one who believes in me, even if he dies, will live.
—John 11:25 (NIV)

Affirmation/prayer: Belief is the core of my successes and failures. If I am to succeed, I must first believe that I can. Jesus, help my unbelief when it comes to living in this world. Help any unbelief in you, the only one who can give me eternal life.

God is my source!

August 26

MY STEPS

The LORD directs the steps of the godly. He delights in every detail of their lives. Though they stumble, they will never fall, for the LORD holds them by the hand.
—Psalms 37:23–24 (NLT)

Affirmation/prayer: I will not discount my days of little steps. Big steps, little steps, or stumbles, I will get where God wants me to be. Lord, hold my hands.

God is my source!

August 27

NO MATTER WHAT

Give thanks to the Lord, for he is good; his love endures forever.
—1 Chronicles 16:34 (NIV)

But God demonstrates his own love for us in this: While we were still sinners, Christ died for us.
—Romans 5:8 (NIV)

Affirmation/prayer: Thank you, Lord, for a love that endures forever. Your love does not give up on me. I pray for forgiveness of sins. Thank you for a love that compels me to turn to you even in my darkest hour, no matter what.

God is my source!

August 28

IT'S ALL GOOD

Every good and perfect gift is from above, coming down from the Father of the heavenly lights, who does not change like shifting shadows.
—James 1:17 (NIV)

Affirmation/prayer: Every single good thing that I have comes from above. Sometimes God uses me to pass his goodness on to others.

God is my source, and that will never change!

August 29

ETERNAL GOD

Before the mountains were born or you brought forth the whole world, from everlasting to everlasting you are God.
—Psalms 90:2 (NIV)

Affirmation/prayer: When I take myself out of the equation, God is still God. I remove my limited view of God when I don't view him for what He can do for me or I for Him. When I go beyond my wants or need, I see clearly a powerful, ever-lasting-to-everlasting God. Praise his holy and eternal name!

God is my source!

August 30

SELF-AWARENESS

I have considered my conduct, and I promise to follow your instructions. Without delay I hurry to obey your commands.
—Psalms 119:59–60 (GNT)

Affirmation/prayer: Lord, as I examine my lifestyle today, show me the ways that stand in my way of living the good life you have set before me. I humbly ask that you remove hidden doubts, fears, and any sins that block me from seeing the gifts and talents you have given me. Let me not procrastinate to make the necessary changes needed for my growth. Use me according to your will so that I may serve you and those you have placed in my life. Thank you for being my source on this journey of self-awareness and growth.

God is my source!

August 31

BROKENHEARTED

He heals the brokenhearted and binds up their wounds.
—Psalms 147:3 (NIC)

The LORD is close to the brokenhearted and saves those who are crushed in spirit.
—Psalms 34:18 (NIV)

Affirmation/prayer: Having many problems to deal with in this world will sometimes leave me heartbroken, disappointed, or even grief stricken. When my heart breaks, Jesus, you are the first to know. Bandage and heal anything in me that is broken. Thank you for your healing power that restores me. Jesus, I feel your love every day.

I will say to myself, "Cheer up; these feelings won't last always. Every road comes to an end."

God is my source!

September

September 1

I AM WILLING

Beside the pool was a man who had been sick for 38 years. When Jesus saw the man and realized that he had been crippled for a long time, he asked him, "Do you want to be healed?"
—John 5:5–6 (CEV)

For I can do everything through Christ, who gives me strength.
—Philippians 4:13 (NLT)

Affirmation/prayer: Sometimes the only things that stand in my way of letting God solve my problems are my ego, pride, and overall defiance. When I am willing, Jesus heals me, solves my problems, and gives me the faith, strength, and courage to walk on. Jesus, I am willing, so please lead me and guide me today, for in you, all things are possible!

God is my source!

September 2

TRIBULATIONS

And not only so, but we glory in tribulations also: knowing that tribulation worketh patience; And patience, experience; and experience, hope.
—Romans 5:3–4 (KJV)

Affirmation/prayer: Jesus, your word tells me that all of my experiences in life will not be happy ones. Yet I know that I can learn from everything that happens, good or bad. Help me to be patient when suffering and trials arise. I ask for the faith that I don't give up. May I have the courage to lean on you, no matter what. Yesterday's problems taught me that just when I think all is lost, the answer always comes with your gifts of patience, experience, and hope. Thank you, Jesus, for today's problems that teach me patience, experience, and hope.

God is my source!

September 3

A THANKFUL HEART

Praise the Lord, my soul, and forget not all his benefits—who forgives all your sins and heals all your diseases, who redeems your life from the pit and crowns you with love and compassion, who satisfies your desires with good thing, so that your youth is renewed like the eagle's.
—Psalms 103:2–5 (NIV)

Affirmation/prayer: Instead of complaining about the things I do not have, I thank you, Lord, for my blessings. Lord, give me a thankful heart so that I may not forget or ignore the good things you do for me daily. Give me a heart of mercy so these good things may flow from me to others.

God is my source!

September 4

CLOUD COVERAGE

But you were like a cloud, protecting us from the sun. You kept our enemies from singing songs of victory.

The LORD All-Powerful will destroy the power of death and wipe away all tears.
—Isaiah 25:5, 8 (CEV)

Affirmation/prayer: Lord, you cover me like a cloud so that I don't feel the heat from the rhetoric of my enemies. Jesus, you feel my sorrows and wipe my tears away. You have promised me I need not fear anything, not even death. I am grateful that you cover me like a cloud on a hot summer day.

God is my source!

September 5

HE GIVES ME JOY

May the God of hope fill you with all joy and peace as you trust in him, so that you may overflow with hope by the power of the Holy Spirit.
—Romans 15:13

Though you have not seen him, you love him; and even though you do not see him now, you believe in him and are filled with an inexpressible and glorious joy.
—1 Peter 1:8–9 (NIV)

Affirmation/prayer: Thank Jesus, who has placed overflowing love and joy in my heart. Today I will let his joy and love overflow from me to others.

God is my source!

September 6

THE TRUE VINE

Jesus said I am the vine; you are the branches. If you remain in me and I in you, you will bear much fruit; apart from me you can do nothing.
—John 15:5 (NIV)

Affirmation/prayer: Jesus, please remove anything in my heart that separates me from you. Please don't let me attach myself to things that are worthless. Apart from you, I am lost, and life is meaningless. With you, I am blessed. With you, I able to serve and bless others.

God is my source!

September 7

AMAZING GRACE

But after you have suffered for a little while, the God of all grace, who calls you to share his eternal glory in union with Christ, will himself perfect you and give you firmness, strength, and a sure foundation.
—1 Peter 5:10 (GNT)

And now I commend you to the care of God and to the message of his grace, which is able to build you up and give you the blessings God has for all his people.
—Acts 20:32 (GNT)

Affirmation/prayer: Thank you, Lord, for your grace that looks beyond my faults and human frailties. I stand firm in this world because your grace restores, confirms, strengthens, and provides for me a sure foundation daily.

Therefore I will not fear but live confidently knowing that your grace and mercy are with me today and eternally. Thank you for loving me, Jesus, and for amazing grace.

God is my source!

September 8

PRAISE

Praise the LORD, my soul, and forget not all his benefits.
—Psalms 103:2 (NIV)

Give thanks to the Lord, for he is good; his love endures forever.
—1 Chronicles 16:34 (NIV)

From the rising of the sun to the place where it sets, the name of the LORD is to be praised.
—Psalms 113:3 (NIV)

Affirmation/prayer: Praising God gets me out of self-pity. Praising God refreshes my memory of how far God has brought me. Lord, praise you for being so good and kind to me. My heart sings when I think of all of the good things that you have done for me. Thank you, Lord, for giving me a love that lasts forever.

God is my source!

September 9

MY FRIEND

For who is God besides the LORD? And who is the Rock except our God? It is God who arms me with strength and keeps my way secure.
—2 Samuel 22:32–33 (NIV)

I have called you friends, for everything that I learned from my Father I have made known to you.
—John 15:15 (NIV)

Affirmation/prayer: Thank you, Lord, for being my friend. You are my strength, my rock, my guide, and a friend who is with me each day.

God is my source!

September 10

DEEP WATERS

He reached down from on high and took hold of me; he drew me out of deep waters. He rescued me from my powerful enemy, from my foes, who were too strong for me.

He brought me out into a spacious place; he rescued me because he delighted in me.
—2 Samuel 22:17–18, 20 (NIV)

Affirmation/prayer: When life gets the best of me and I feel like I am drowning in deep water, God steps in, pulls me up, and puts me on dry ground. Thank you, Lord, for your hand that saves me when problems arise and my enemies are getting the best of me. Help me to remember that there is no problem too deep for you to handle.

God is my source!

September 11

WELL DONE

For God is not unjust. He will not forget how hard you have worked for him and how you have shown your love to him by caring for other believers, as you still do.
—Hebrews 6:10 (NLT)

Affirmation/prayer: Thank you, Lord, that you have blessed me to be able to serve you and others. Use me to continue to spread your love. When it seems family or friends do not appreciate the good I do or even care, may I hear your voice saying to me, "Well done, my child, well done."

God is my source!

September 12

FLOURISHING LIKE AN OLIVE TREE

But I am like an olive tree flourishing in the house of God; I trust in God's unfailing love for ever and ever.
—Psalms 52:8 (NIV)

Affirmation/prayer: The love of God sustains me. Like the sap of an olive tree, his love for me daily is a renewed source of vigor and vitality. I am safe and happy because I trust God to take care of me forever and ever. Thank you, Lord, for loving me.

God is my source!

September 13

WAIT AND BE STRONG

Wait for the LORD; Be strong and let your heart take courage; Yes, wait for the LORD.
—Psalms 27:14 (ESV)

Lead me in your truth and teach me, for you are the God of my salvation; for you I wait all the day long.
—Psalms 25:5 (ESV)

Affirmation/prayer: Lord, when I read your word, I find the wisdom that teaches me to wait on you. Lord, help me to get out of self-will and wait on you. Waiting patiently on you removes all fear and doubt, which frees my mind to concentrate on solutions, not problems. Lord, please give me courage to move on when things don't go my way. Thank you for teaching me how to wait on thee.

God is my source!

September 14

NEED, NOT GREED

And we are confident that he hears us whenever we ask for anything that pleases him. And since we know he hears us when we make our requests, we also know that he will give us what we ask for.
—1 John 5:14–15 (NLT)

Affirmation/prayer: Thank you, Lord, for hearing my prayers. As I pray, may I seek your will for my life. Help me remember that you will meet the need, not the greed.

God is my source!

September 15

SEEK MY FACE

When you said, Seek my face; my heart said unto you, your face, LORD, will I seek.
—Psalms 27:8 (NIV)

Affirmation/prayer: Lord, in my heart I hear you say to me, "Pray about it." Thank you for your voice within that speaks to me. When I pray about life, you guide and strengthen me. I feel your love as I turn to you in prayer. May I always remember to pray and call on your name.

God is my source!

September 16

FIRST THINGS FIRST

Don't worry or ask yourselves "Will we have anything to eat?"
"Will we have anything to drink?" or "What will we wear?"
Only people who don't know God are always worrying about such
things. Your Father in heaven knows you need all of these. But
more than anything else, put God's work first and do what he
wants. Then the other things will be yours as well.
—Matthew 6:31–33 (CEV)

Affirmation/prayer: How about I start every day seeking God in prayer and meditation, asking, "Not my will but thy will be done?" Lord, you have shown me that when I put you first, everything else falls into place. I need not worry because I know that it is you, God, not me who is supplying all my needs. Jesus, please help me keep you first in my life. Amen!

God is my source!

September 17

YET I WILL REJOICE

Although the fig tree shall not blossom, neither shall fruit be in the vines; the labour of the olive shall fail, and the fields shall yield no meat; the flock shall be cut off from the fold, and there shall be no herd in the stalls: Yet I will rejoice in the LORD, I will joy in the God of my salvation. The LORD God is my strength.
—Habakkuk 3:17–19 (KJV)

Affirmation/prayer: Lord, help me not look at and be discouraged by the things that are going wrong in my life. As your child, let me rejoice in you. My hope, desires, and confidence are in knowing that you, Jesus, did not bring me this far to leave me. I will rejoice and have joy in the Lord. The Lord is my strength!

God is my source!

September 18

CHANGE

You were told that your foolish desires will destroy you and that you must give up your old way of life with all its bad habits. Let the Spirit change your way of thinking and make you into a new person. You were created to be like God.
—Ephesians 4:22–24 (CEV)

Jesus told him, "Pick up your mat and walk!"
—John 5:8 (CEV)

Affirmation/prayer: I will do my part to put off the old habits that destroy my mind, body, and soul. If I want God to change me, I must participate. Lord, give me the courage to move away from the old way of life and bad habits that destroy the mind, body, and soul. Holy Spirit, please change my way of thinking.

God is my source!

September 19

TRUTH

Test me, LORD, and try me, examine my heart and my mind; for I have always been mindful of your unfailing love and have lived in reliance on your faithfulness.
—Psalms 26:2–3 (NIV)

I have considered my ways and have turned my steps to your statutes.
—Psalms 119:59 (NIV)

Affirmation/prayer: Lord, help me to examine my truths. Only then can I change the *what*, *when*, and *why* I do the things that I do. May your unfailing love lead me in all my affairs to be truthful to you, myself, and others.

God is my source!

September 20

DELIVER ME

In times of trouble, may the LORD answer your cry.

May he grant your heart's desires and make all your plans succeed.
May the LORD answer all your prayers.
—Psalms 20:1, 4–5 (NLT)

Affirmation/prayer: Trouble will come to me in this life. Lord, help me and deliver me through troublesome times. Without your power and strength, I can't make it in this world. The desires of my heart are given to me according to your will. I eagerly sing praises of how you can and will deliver.

God is my source!

September 21

INEXPERIENCE AND FOOLISHNESS

Leave inexperience behind, and you will live; pursue the way of understanding.

Instruct the wise, and he will be wiser still; teach the righteous, and he will learn more. The fear of the LORD is the beginning of wisdom.
—Proverbs 9:6, 9–10 (CSB)

Affirmation/prayer: Lord, you know that I have suffered the consequences of my inexperience and foolishness many times. The thought that I can handle everything on my own is foolishness. In all my affairs, where I lack knowledge, Lord please give me wisdom.

Lord, give me wisdom!

God is my source!

September 22

JUST RELAX: SELF-CONTROL

Who is slow to anger is better than the mighty, And he who rules his spirit, than he who captures a city.
—Proverbs 16:32 (NASB)

Your will be done, On earth as it is in heaven.
—Matthew 6:10 (NASB)

Affirmation/prayer: Lord, sometimes I get angry, upset, anxious, and stressed out trying to work things out in my own spirit and timing. In these times, help me to control my thoughts and actions. Please help me to slow down, relax and just say, "Thy will be done."

God is my source!

September 23

ABUNDANT LIFE

I pray that out of his glorious riches he may strengthen you with power through his Spirit in your inner being.

Now to him who is able to do immeasurably more than all we ask or imagine, according to his power that is at work within us.
—Ephesians 3:16, 20 (NIV)

Affirmation/prayer: Jesus, may I not rely on my own power but your power within me. Take control of my life. Do not let my ego and pride stop me from tapping your power within me. You are able to do for me above and beyond everything I can ever ask or think. To you I give the glory. Amen!

God is my source!

September 24

OPTIMISTIC

This is the day the LORD has made. We will rejoice and be glad in it.
—Psalms 118:24 (NLT)

Rejoice in our confident hope. Be patient in trouble, and keep on praying.
—Romans 12:12 (NLT)

Affirmation/prayer: I will look on the bright side of life. I am rejoicing and thanking God for every promise he has given me. I am rejoicing and thanking God for the blessings, love, and hope that will come my way. If trouble arises this day, I am optimistic, knowing that God has all the answers to my problems.

God is my source!

September 25

BATTLES

Wisdom brings strength, and knowledge gives power. Battles are won by listening to advice and making a lot of plans.
—Proverbs 24:5–6 (CEV)

Affirmation/prayer: Lord, at home or work, or in social settings, when problems arise, please remove foolishness from my heart so that I may seek wise, godly counsel before I act. Please point me to wise, godly counselors when problems arise. Isaiah 9:6 says that you are a Wonderful Counselor. Thank you, Lord, for your word, which helps me live me a powerful and victorious life.

God is my source!

September 26

GOD

For the LORD your God is the God of all gods, the LORD of all lords, the great God, mighty and awesome, who does not show favoritism or take bribes.
—Deuteronomy 10:17 (NIV)

Affirmation/prayer: Lord, I praise you because you are God over everything. You can't be bribed, so I am glad to call you my friend. You are no respecter of person; therefore, I will not fear anyone or anything. I will put my trust in you. You are my protector and my provider. God, you are all I need!

God is my source!

September 28

OVERCOMING UNBELIEF

Immediately the boy's father exclaimed, "I do believe, but help me overcome my unbelief!"
—Mark 9:24 (NIV)

Do not let your hearts be troubled. You believe in God; believe also in me.
—John 14:1 (NIV)

Now faith is confidence in what we hope for and assurance about what we do not see.
—Hebrews 11:1 (NIV)

Affirmation/prayer: When I lack faith and hope, it is because of my unbelieving spirit. Today I will overcome my unbelief by asking for God's help. I will not let worry take first place when I don't have all the answers. I will read his word and hold on to his promises. Believing and putting my faith in Jesus is the overall cure for overcoming my unbelief. Jesus, help my unbelief.

God is my source!

September 29

GET A GOOD UNDERSTANDING

Get wisdom, get understanding; do not forget my words or turn away from them. Do not forsake wisdom, and she will protect you; love her, and she will watch over you. The beginning of wisdom is this: Get wisdom. Though it cost all you have, get understanding.
—Proverbs 4:5–7 (NIV)

Affirmation/prayer: Lord, before I speak or do anything today, help me to get a good understanding. Amen.

God is my source!

September 29

JEALOUSY

A peaceful heart leads to a healthy body; jealousy is like cancer in the bones.
—Proverbs 14:30 (NLT)

Surely resentment destroys the fool, and jealousy kills the simple.
—Job 5:2 (NLT)

Love is patient and kind. Love is not jealous or boastful or proud.
—1 Corinthians 13:4 (NLT)

Affirmation/prayer: Lord, please keep the spirit of jealousy away from me. There will always be those that have more than I. There will always be those that have less than I. When I am jealous of those with more, it destroys my mind body and soul. When I boast of what I have, it may spur up the spirit of jealousy in others. Help me keep my ego and pride in check with your love. Love does not boast, keep score, or envy others.

God is my source!

September 30

CHARGE MY BATTERIES

Yet the news about him spread all the more, so that crowds of people came to hear him and to be healed of their sicknesses. But Jesus often withdrew to lonely places and prayed.
—Luke 5:15–16 (NIV)

Affirmation/prayer: Jesus, you are my example of the importance of prayer and the need to take time to be recharged. Help me today to slow down and take the time to pray and meditate. Without your strength and power, I cannot go on. Please guide me in living a life that includes you in prayer and meditation. I need your strength and power. Please charge my batteries!

God is my source!

October

October 1

SEEKING HIS MERCY

Hear me as I pray, O LORD. Be merciful and answer me! My heart has heard you say, "Come and talk with me." And my heart responds, "LORD, I am coming."
—Psalms 27:7–8 (NLT)

My dear children, I am writing this to you so that you will not sin. But if anyone does sin, we have an advocate who pleads our case before the Father. He is Jesus Christ, the one who is truly righteous.
—1 John 2:1 (NLT)

Affirmation/prayer: Jesus, I hear your voice telling me to come and talk to you about my problems, mistakes, and sins. My heart is responding to the call when I am approaching your throne of grace and asking for your mercy. Jesus, please help me to overcome anything that defeats me. Please forgive me for my sins. Thank you for your love, grace, and mercy.

God is my source!

October 2

BOUNDARIES

LORD, you alone are my portion and my cup; you make my lot secure. The boundary lines have fallen for me in pleasant places; surely I have a delightful inheritance. I will praise the LORD, who counsels me; even at night my heart instructs me.
—Psalms 16:5–7 (NIV)

Affirmation/prayer: Lord, you have set wonderful boundaries for me drawn out of your love. Even at night, you speak to me and counsel me because you love me. Show me how to use your boundaries to paint a beautiful picture of my life. Teach me how to set boundaries in all areas of my life—physical, emotional, and spiritual. I praise you, Lord, because you not only provide for me, but your boundary lines also keep me safe and secure.

God is my source!

October 3

ROADS

Enter through the narrow gate. For wide is the gate and broad is the road that leads to destruction, and many enter through it. But small is the gate and narrow the road that leads to life, and only a few find it.
—Matthew 7:13–14 (NIV)

Affirmation/prayer: Lord, help me remember that the road to success is often a narrow one. The road to eternal life is even narrower. May I not be surprised at times when I am doing my best that no one is standing beside me but you.

God is my source!

October 4

FORGIVENESS

Forgive us the wrongs we have done, as we forgive the wrongs that others have done to us. Do not bring us to hard testing, but keep us safe from the Evil One. If you forgive others the wrongs they have done to you, your Father in heaven will also forgive you. But if you do not forgive others, then your Father will not forgive the wrongs you have done.
—Matthew 6:12–15 (GNT)

Affirmation/prayer: Lord, one of the hardest tests in my life is forgiving others, especially when I feel that I did not deserve the treatment. I humbly ask for the wisdom and strength to forgive those who have and will offend me. Your word tells me no one is without offense (Rom. 3:23).

Please keep me from the traps of the evil one (e.g., shame, guilt, and low self-esteem) by loving you first, myself next, and others when forgiving. Give me your wisdom to set healthy boundaries with those who constantly offend. Give me an extra dose of your love so that I may always have a forgiving heart. Thank you, Jesus, for dying so that I can have your forgiveness of my sins.

God is my source!

October 5

IT'S FOR MY GOOD

And now, Israel, what doth the LORD thy God require of thee, but to fear the LORD thy God, to walk in all his ways, and to love him, and to serve the LORD thy God with all thy heart and with all thy soul, and to observe the LORD's commands and decrees that I am giving you today for your own good?
—Deuteronomy 10:12–13 (ESV)

And you shall love the Lord your God with all your heart and with all your soul and with all your mind and with all your strength.
—Mark 12:30 (ESV)

Affirmation/prayer: Your words teach me to give to you:
my love,
my respect,
my actions,
my heart,
my all.
It's for my good.

God is my source!

October 6

DECISIONS

Seek his will in all you do, and he will show you which path to take.
—Proverbs 3:6 (NLT)

We can make our plans, but the LORD determines our steps.
—Proverbs 16:9 (NLT)

Affirmation/prayer: I can trust myself to make the right decisions with God's help. Please, Lord, give me clear directions this day.

God is my source!

October 7

UNDESERVED GRACE

But God treated me with undeserved grace! He made me what I am, and his grace wasn't wasted. I worked much harder than any of the other apostles, although it was really God's grace at work and not me.
—1 Corinthians 15:10 (CEV)

Affirmation/prayer: The same grace and mercy given to Paul is available to me today. Lord, please help me to walk in your grace daily. It is not by works, but it is through your grace and mercy that I succeed. It is your grace and mercy that keeps me motivated to go on when all else fails.

God, you are my source!

October 8

LOVING EYES

I will instruct you and teach you in the way you should go; I will counsel you with my loving eye on you.
—Psalms 32:8 (NIV)

But the eyes of the LORD are on those who fear him, on those whose hope is in his unfailing love.
—Psalms 33:18 (NIV)

Affirmation/prayer: God's loving eyes are watching over me. All he asks of me is to follow his lead and put my trust and hope in his unfailing love.

God is my source!

October 9

HOW TO SUCCEED

Then the LORD told me: "I will give you my message in the form of a vision. Write it clearly enough to be read at a glance. At the time I have decided, my words will come true. You can trust what I say about the future. It may take a long time, but keep on waiting—it will happen! I, the LORD, refuse to accept anyone who is proud. Only those who live by faith are acceptable to me."
—Habakkuk 2:2–4 (CEV)

Affirmation/prayer: Reading and following God's word in the Bible is the very thing I need to succeed.

How to Succeed:
1. Align my goals with God's word.
2. Write them down.
3. Believe his word is true.
4. Ask God to help me move beyond my thoughts and my limited vision.
5. Don't let weaknesses blind me. Keep the Faith.
6. Remember that it is written that God does not answer in my time, but in the time he sees best for me.
7. Keep ego in check focusing on God's power and promises so as to remain at peace.
8. Keep ego in check by honoring God when I succeed.
9. Keep the faith knowing that the righteous one succeed
10. Remember: God is my source!

October 10

MY CUP OVERFLOWS

The LORD is my shepherd; I have all that I need.

You prepare a feast for me in the presence of my enemies. You honor me by anointing my head with oil. My cup overflows with blessings. Surely your goodness and unfailing love will pursue me all the days of my life, and I will live in the house of the LORD forever.
—Psalms 23:1, 5–6 (NLT)

Affirmation/prayer: Lord, thank you for overflowing my life with your blessings. The food I waste, clothes I don't wear, and stuff that I call excess or junk—Lord, you call it overflowing my cup. Help me grateful by sharing your goodness, mercy, unfailing love, and your overflow with others.

God is my source!

October 11

ONE WHO EXAMINES

You have tested my thoughts and examined my heart in the night. You have scrutinized me and found nothing wrong. I am determined not to sin in what I say.
—Psalms 17:3 (NLT)

God is my shield, saving those whose hearts are true and right.
—Psalms 7:10 (NLT)

Affirmation/prayer: Jesus, I find comfort in knowing that you know and empathize with my deepest thoughts and emotions. You taught me that I don't know what anyone is thinking, but you do! You see the good and evil in everyone. Keep my thoughts pure as I deal with my enemies. You are righteous. You are my source, my strength, and my shield.

God is my source!

October 12

GOD IS NEAR

God has done all this, so that we will look for him and reach out and find him. He isn't far from any of us, and he gives us the power to live, to move, and to be who we are. "We are his children," just as some of your poets have said.
—Acts 17:28–28 (CEV)

Affirmation/prayer: Thank you, Jesus, that you are not some distant God far off in the universe. Your spirit dwells inside me and empowers me with life. I am Your child; therefore, I can depend on you to be near when I call out to you.

God is my source!

October 13

WIN OR LOSE

He said, "I came naked from my mother's womb, and I will be naked when I leave. The LORD gave me what I had, and the LORD has taken it away. Praise the name of the LORD!"
—Job 1:21

Affirmation/prayer: This verse helps me put life in perspective. It helps me deal with my wins and my failures. Those who know me only by what I own or prestige do not know the real me. Looking away from the things of this world and to you Lord, I find peace. I have learned how to live life and grow whether I win or lose.

God is my source!

October 14

OPINIONS

Trust in the LORD with all your heart; do not depend on your own understanding. Seek his will in all you do, and he will show you which path to take.
—Proverbs 3:5–6 (NLT)

Affirmation/prayer: My opinions are no good if they do not line up with the truth. Lord, give me the wisdom and desire to seek your will in making all my decisions.

God is my source!

October 15

SIN

Therefore, since we are surrounded by such a huge crowd of witnesses to the life of faith, let us strip off every weight that slows us down, especially the sin that so easily trips us up. And let us run with endurance the race God has set before us.
—Hebrews 12:1 (NLT)

Affirmation/prayer: Lord, help me get rid of the hidden things and sins that are holding me back. Before I sin in mind, body, spirit, or soul, give me the wisdom to know that such things will cost me more than I want to pay. Even if all others fail me, give me the courage and faith not to give into my sins and keep running my race. To God be the glory!

God is my source!

October 16

MY TRUE REWARD

The LORD is with you when you are with him. If you seek him, he will be found by you, but if you forsake him, he will forsake you.

But as for you, be strong and do not give up, for your work will be rewarded.
—2 Chronicles 15:2, 7 (NLT)

Affirmation/prayer: Lord, please be with me today, as you were with your children in past times. Please help me cling to you. Help me to not be discouraged in difficult times but work on knowing my true reward comes from you.

God is my source!

October 17

GIVING

Don't look out only for your own interests, but take an interest in others, too. You must have the same attitude that Christ Jesus had.
—Philippians 2:4–5 (NLT)

You should remember the words of the Lord Jesus: "It is more blessed to give than to receive."
—Acts 20:35 (NLT)

Affirmation/prayer: Lord, where there is need, please open my eyes to see where and I may help. Jesus, show me how to bless others through giving. Jesus, show me how to serve others.

God is my source!

October 18

PLANS

"For I know the plans I have for you," declares the LORD, "plans to prosper you and not to harm you, plans to give you hope and a future."
—Jeremiah 29:11 (NIV)

Affirmation/prayer: Lord, in you, I function at my best in mind, body, spirit, and soul. Help me cling to your plan for my life, which is filled with hope and prosperity. Your plan is not one of negative restrictions but a plan that frees me of the things that cripple me. Lord, life can leave me misguided and confused. When I'm in doubt, show me the way.

God is my source!

October 19

ASK FOR THE OLD WAY

This is what the LORD says: "Stop at the crossroads and look around. Ask for the old, godly way, and walk in it. Travel its path, and you will find rest for your souls. But you reply, 'No, that's not the road we want!'"
—Jeremiah 6:16

Teach me your ways, O LORD, that I may live according to your truth! Grant me purity of heart, so that I may honor you.
—Psalms 86:11 (NLT)

Affirmation/prayer: When I am at a crossroads and don't know how to go on, it is a good time to hit the pause button. It is time to remember that the path that the word of God put in place long ago is still able to lead and guide me today. When I am angry, upset, depressed, anxious, agitated, and confused, I will go back to God's word. I will meditate, focus, and hang on to its every word. I will walk in its truth and honor God.

God is my source!

October 20

WHO AM I?

Behave like obedient children. Don't let your lives be controlled by your desires, as they used to be. Always live as God's holy people should, because God is the one who chose you, and he is holy.

—1 Peter 1:14–15 (CEV)

Affirmation/prayer: Lord you are holy, loving, and kind to me. Please help me be holy, loving, and kind to others. Don't let me give in to my fleshly desires when I am dealing with those around me. May I remember that following your lead speaks louder of who I truly am than the words I speak. May I lovingly always remember that I am your child. Amen.

God is my source!

October 21

PEACE

Peace with God

Therefore, since we have been made right in God's sight by faith, we have peace with God because of what Jesus Christ our Lord has done for us.
—Romans 5:1 (NLT)

Peace of God

You will keep in perfect peace all who trust in you, all whose thoughts are fixed on you!
—Isaiah 26:3 (NLT)

Affirmation/prayer: Jesus, please help me look beyond this ever-changing world and put my trust in you. No matter what today brings, you give me peace when I focus my thoughts on you and your love for me.

God is my source!

October 22

PEP TALK

As soon as I pray, you answer me; you encourage me by giving me strength.
—Psalms 138:3 (NLT)

Affirmation/prayer: Pep talks are used to create enthusiasm and encourage. Lord, your words do just that. All I need to do is listen.

"I Got You"
....Be strong and courageous... Do not be afraid; do not be discouraged, for the LORD your God will be with you wherever you go."
—Joshua 1:9 (NIV)

"You Can Do This"
I can do all things through him who gives me strength.
—Philippians 4:13 (NIV)

"I Am with You"
....Never will I leave you or forsake you.
—Hebrews 13:5 (NIV)

God is my source!

October 23

HAPPY THOUGHTS

Rejoice in the Lord always. I will say it again: Rejoice!
—Philippians 4:4

Praise the LORD, my soul, and forget not all his benefits who forgives all your sins and heals all your diseases, who redeems your life from the pit and crowns you with love and compassion.
—Psalms 103:2–4 (NIV)

Affirmation/prayer: I am happy when I get out of myself and think on the goodness of God. Praise you, Lord. My heart rejoices knowing that I can pray to you about everything. I will always remember to count my blessings. A thankful heart and happy thoughts go hand in hand.

God is my source!

October 24

HOPES AND DREAMS

"The LORD is my portion," says my soul, "therefore I hope in Him."
—Lamentations 3:24 (ESV)

Affirmation/prayer: Lord, the one joy you have given my soul is the ability to hope and dream. Thank you for inspiring me to hope and dream about the good things you have in store for me. May I never lose hope in you and your goodness. Give me the courage to keep on hoping and dreaming and working to make my dreams come true. Thy will be done. Amen.

God is my source!

October 25

MY SHEPHERD

You, LORD, are my shepherd. I will never be in need. You let me rest in fields of green grass. You lead me to streams of peaceful water, and you refresh my life. You are true to your name, and you lead me along the right paths. I may walk through valleys as dark as death, but I won't be afraid. You are with me, and your shepherd's rod makes me feel safe. You treat me to a feast, while my enemies watch. You honor me as your guest, and you fill my cup until it overflows. Your kindness and love will always be with me each day of my life, and I will live forever in your house, LORD.
—Psalms 23:1-6 (CSV)

Affirmation/prayer: God's word assures me, refreshes me, renews me, leads me, comforts me, and gives me hope. Surely the Lord is my shepherd.

God is my source!

October 26

OWNING MY POWER

God's Spirit doesn't make cowards out of us. The Spirit gives us power, love, and self-control.
—2 Timothy 1:7 (CEV)

Affirmation/prayer: I do not have to give other people's actions the power to send me into a tailspin and ruin my day. God has given me power to not fear. When I am faced with the actions of selfish, angry, shaming, or even loving people, my response is my choice. Lord, today help me look to your spirit (power) within so I won't give others the power to control my day.

God is my source!

October 27

HAPPINESS

As the Father hath loved me, so have I loved you: continue ye in my love.
—John 15:9 (KJV)

Affirmation/prayer: Good and bad times come and go, but the only real and lasting happiness is loving others and myself. Jesus, help me continue in your love.

God is my source!

October 28

GOD IS WITH ME

You have kept count of my wanderings. Put my tears in your bottle—have not you recorded them in your book? Then my enemies will retreat on the day when I call. This I know: God is for me.

In God I trust; I will not fear. What can man do to me?
—Psalms 56:8–9, 11 (HCSB)

Affirmation/prayer: I will face my enemies head-on knowing that God is so close to me that he sees every tear I shed. Lord, not only do you know what I go through in this life, but you have also counted each and every step of my being. At home, work, or play, I will trust you to handle the things that come against me. I have experienced your deliverance in the past. Now I am not afraid when I pray, and I trust you.

God is my source!

October 29

OVERCOMING SIN

Well then, should we keep on sinning so that God can show us more and more of his wonderful grace? Of course not! Since we have died to sin, how can we continue to live in it?

We know that our old sinful selves were crucified with Christ so that sin might lose its power in our lives. We are no longer slaves to sin. For when we died with Christ, we were set free from the power of sin.

Do not let sin control the way you live; do not give in to sinful desires.
—Romans 6:1–2, 6–7, 12 (NLT)

Affirmation/prayer: Old habits die hard. Bad habits such as lying, stealing, getting drunk, gossiping, overspending—over-anything—are habits that destroy the self. Jesus did not give me his forgiveness and grace so that I can be a slave to myself. His love compels me to live a righteous life. His power gives me the strength to do just that.

God is my source!

October 30

LIMITLESS GOD

Yet I am always with you; you hold me by my right hand. You guide me with your counsel, and afterward you will take me into glory.
—Psalms 73:23–24 (NIV)

Affirmation/prayer: My prayers are not limited to this earthly realm. Thank you, God, for the power of prayer. My prayers go up to heaven, and you fill me with wisdom and knowledge from above. You are a limitless God who is with me on earth and will be with me in the life to come.

God is my source!

October 31

A DIFFERENT MIND-SET

Is the glass half full or half empty?
—Old saying

And now, dear brothers and sisters, one final thing. Fix your thoughts on what is true, and honorable, and right, and pure, and lovely, and admirable. Think about things that are excellent and worthy of praise.
—Philippians 4:8 (NLT)

Affirmation/prayer: My thoughts control whether I see more positive than negative, more hope than defeat, more joy than sadness, more peace than confusion. I may not be in control of the situation, but I can train my mind through meditation and prayer to look on the positive side of life. My giant becomes smaller and is just one more thing that I can handle when I give it to you, Lord.

God is my source!

November

November 1

WILLING

When a man's willing and eager, God joins in.
—Aeschylus

So I say to you: Ask and it will be given to you; seek and you will find; knock and the door will be opened to you.
—Luke 11:9 (NIV)

Affirmation/prayer: I know, Lord, that you are with me. Help me today to do all that I have to do. Thy will be done.

God is my source!

November 2

LIGHT VERSUS DARKNESS

For once you were full of darkness, but now you have light from the Lord. So live as people of light! For this light within you produces only what is good and right and true.

For the light makes everything visible. This is why it is said, "Awake, O sleeper, rise up from the dead, and Christ will give you light."
—Ephesians 5:8–9, 14 (NLT)

Affirmation/prayer: It is written that "darkness is the absence of light."

Thank you, Jesus, for the God-given light I have within. I can see the road ahead and avoid many pitfalls when I remember to let this light within guide me. Please help this light within me shine so brightly that I may live a life that shows your goodness, righteousness, and truth.

God is my source!

November 3

BUT GOD

But by the grace of God I am what I am...
—1 Corinthians 15:10

But because of his great love for us, God, who is rich in mercy, made us alive with Christ even when we were dead in transgressions—it is by grace you have been saved.
—Ephesians 2:4–5 (NIV)

Affirmation/prayer: Lord, I praise you for the love and mercy you have shown me. When I look at my life, I recognize that it is you who has kept me and not me. You did not do it because I did something to deserve it but simply because of your love for me. Every day, give me enough love and wisdom to remember that only by the grace of God am I what I am, instead of judging others for their mistakes.

God is my source!

November 4

WISDOM AND KNOWLEDGE

A wise man *will hear, and will increase learning; and a man of understanding shall attain unto wise counsels.*
—Proverbs 1:5 (NASB)

The heart of the discerning acquires knowledge, for the ears of the wise seek it out.
—Proverbs 18:15 (NIV)

Affirmation/prayer: Just because I can do something does not mean that I should do it. There is such a thing as "cause and effect" in life. Lord, I pray for wisdom, knowledge, and wise counsel in matters of health, wealth, relationships, family, and so forth. I pray that my decisions are a blessing for me and others.

God is my source!

November 5

I WILL TRUST IN YOU

Those who know your name trust in you, for you, LORD, have never forsaken those who seek you.
—Psalms 9:10 (NIV)

But I trust in you, LORD; I say, "You are my God."
—Psalms 31:14 (NIV)

Affirmation/prayer: Lord, help me to truly trust in you, not only in my words but also in my actions. You have been so good to me. With every victory and every good thing that you give me, my trust grows deeper and deeper each day. You have held my hands through the good and bad times. Therefore, each day I will say to you, Jesus, "You are my God. I will trust in you."

God is my source!

November 6

JUSTICE LOVE AND HUMILITY

He has shown you, O man, what is good; And what does the LORD require of you But to do justly, To love mercy, And to walk humbly with your God?
—Micah 6:8 (NKJV)

Affirmation/prayer: Lord, please help me put aside ego and pride and put on humility so that I may do what is good. Guide me in the way of justice so that I will treat others fairly. As you give me mercy and love each day, give me the heart to pass love and mercy along to others. Thank you, Jesus, for teaching me that the simple way of doing your will is just to be loving, just, merciful, and humble.

God is my source!

November 7

CHANGE

Not everything that is faced can be changed, but nothing can be changed until it is faced.
—James Baldwin

Keep on asking, and you will receive what you ask for. Keep on seeking, and you will find. Keep on knocking, and the door will be opened to you.
—Matthews 7:7 (NLT)

Affirmation/prayer: Not even God will make changes in my life without me doing something. Even if God gives freely, I must at least receive. Lord, help me do my part in seeking and receiving.

God is my source!

November 8

CLEANSE ME

Purify me from my sins, and I will be clean; wash me, and I will be whiter than snow.

Create in me a clean heart, O God. Renew a loyal spirit within me.
—Psalms 51:7, 10 (NLT)

Affirmation/prayer: Lord, thank you for forgiving my sins. I sin when I don't love you, myself, and others as I should. Please cover my guilt and shame with your love as you change me within. Renew my spirit by changing old thought patterns into new ones. Help me forgive myself. Lord, help me build patience and a steadfast spirit of love and faith in You and me. Lord, cleanse me with your love.

God is my source!

November 9

MY HOPE

Lord, you alone are my hope. I've trusted you, O LORD, from childhood. Yes, you have been with me from birth; from my mother's womb you have cared for me. No wonder I am always praising you!
—Psalms 71:5–6 (NLT)

Affirmation/prayer: Lord, when I think of how you have kept me, I know that you have brought me too far to leave me now. You are my hope.

God is my source!

November 10

GOD CHANGES THINGS

Do not remember the past events, pay no attention to things of old. Look, I am about to do something new; even now it is coming. Do you not see it? Indeed, I will make a way in the wilderness, rivers in the desert.
—Isaiah 43:18–19 (CSB)

Affirmation/prayer: May I not dwell on my past mistakes. Instead, Lord, may I see how you are changing the desert places in my finances, relationships, work, and so forth into rivers of flowing waters each day.

God changes things!

God is my source!

November 11

YOUR LOVE SAVES ME

For God so loved the world that he gave his one and only Son, that whoever believes in him shall not perish but have eternal life. For God did not send his Son into the world to condemn the world, but to save the world through him.
—John 3:16–17 (NIV)

Forgive all our sins and graciously receive us, so that we may offer you our praises.
—Hosea 14:2 (NLT)

Affirmation/prayer: Jesus, because of your love, despite my mistakes, I am never too bad that you cannot save me. Nor will I ever be so good that I can save myself. You do not condemn me, and neither will I spend this day condemning myself for my mistakes. Instead I will live today guided, grounded, and rooted in your love.

God is my source!

November 12

CHOICES

For if ye live after the flesh, ye shall die: but if ye through the Spirit do mortify the deeds of the body, ye shall live.
—Romans 8:13 (KJV)

Affirmation/prayer: I am the one who must take responsibility for my choices. I am the one who will live with the consequences. Jesus, guide me and lead me so that I will not live by others approval or my selfish desires. Life is good when I follow your lead.

God is my source!

November 13

JOY

When anxiety was great within me, your consolation brought me joy.
—Psalms 94:19 (NIV)

Affirmation/prayer: When I am tense, I am letting the things around me strain me mentally and emotionally. My serenity comes from trusting God. The more I trust God, the less tense I am. Lord, help me to trust you in all things great or small. Your consolation brings me joy!

God is my source!

November 14

STRENGTH AND POWER

My health may fail, and my spirit may grow weak, but God remains the strength of my heart; he is mine forever.
—Psalms 73:26 (NLT)

It is not by force nor by strength, but by my Spirit, says the LORD of Heaven's Armies.
—Zechariah 4:6 (NLT)

Affirmation/prayer: Sometimes I feel tired and worn out. Sometimes I am so fearful that my heart tells me to just give up on life. Thank you, Lord, that during these times, your word is a reminder that I accomplish everything because of your strength and the power. Thank you, Lord, for the push of your strength and power that will be with me as long as I live.

God is my source!

November 15

ENCOURAGE ME

May our Lord Jesus Christ himself and God our Father, who loved us and by his grace gave us eternal encouragement and good hope, encourage your hearts and strengthen you in every good deed and word.
—2 Thessalonians 2:16–17(NIV)

Affirmation/prayer: In everything I do today, I will remember that I am empowered by the love of God. Lord, thank you for your loving grace and mercy that encourages me and gives me hope. Strengthen me to do what is best for me and others by saying and doing good things. I ask that you give me all the courage I need to face this day.

God is my source!

November 16

DEPENDING ON GOD

Each time he said, "My grace is all you need. My power works best in weakness." So now I am glad to boast about my weaknesses, so that the power of Christ can work through me. That's why I take pleasure in my weaknesses, and in the insults, hardships, persecutions, and troubles that I suffer for Christ. For when I am weak, then I am strong.
—2 Corinthians 12:9 (NLT)

Affirmation/prayer: I know that understanding my weakness and dependence on God is the beginning of my strength.

God is my source!

November 17

DO IT ENTHUSIASTICALLY

Whatever you do, do it enthusiastically, as something done for the Lord and not for men.
— Colossians 3:23 (HCSB)

Affirmation/prayer: Whatever my task is for today I will do it as working for God. I know that when I do things for people; I may be disappointed. When I do things for God, he never disappoints. Lord, help me work with enthusiasm when it comes to serving you.

God is my source!

November 18

EXPERIENCING LOSS

My days are passed; my plans have been shattered; along with my heart's desires.
— Job 17:11 (ISV)

Because he knows the road on which I travel, when he had tested me, I'll come out like gold.
— Job 23:10 (ISV)

For you know that when your faith is tested, your endurance has a chance to grow. So let it grow, for when your endurance is fully developed, you will be perfect and complete, needing nothing.
— James 1:3-4 (NLT)

Affirmation/prayer: - Lord I can't live life without experiencing loss. When my dreams are shattered. let me not relive those days like broken records. Teach me how to grieve my losses and move on. With you holding my hand I gain strength , wisdom, love joy, and peace even in the midst of losing stuff and the ones I love. All is never lost as long as I have me and a God who loves me.

—

God is my source!

November 19

THANKFULNESS

Praise the LORD. Give thanks to the LORD, for he is good; his love endures forever.
—Psalms 106 (NIV)

Affirmation/prayer: Giving thanks is like taking vitamins to renew my mind and my soul.

Vitamin A: Attitude adjustment. My mind moves from the negative to positive things in my life. I gain faith to move on.

Vitamin B: Blessings. Thanking God for my blessings gives me the strength and courage to face obstacles because I know he has blessed me in good and bad times.

Vitamin C: Counting my blessings and thanking God for them remind me that I serve a God who will supplies all my needs.

Vitamin L: Love—a special vitamin from above. God's love never fails.

A thankful heart is a peaceful heart.

God is my source!

November 20

FEELING EMPTY

You prepare a feast for me in the presence of my enemies. You honor me by anointing my head with oil. My cup overflows with blessings.
—Psalms 23:5 (NLT)

But those who wait upon the LORD will renew their strength.
—Isaiah 40:31 (NLT)

Affirmation/prayer: Lord, as I give to you the things that are not good for me, there may be times when I feel empty. These are the times when you are cleaning and refilling my cup. When I feel empty, give me the courage and strength to press through these feelings and wait on you. Thank you, Lord, as you overflow my cup with good health, good, relationships, and good things.

God is my source!

November 21

ACTIVATE ME LORD

Now to Him who is able to do far more abundantly beyond all that we ask or think, according to the power that works within us.
— Ephesians 3:20 (ESV)

Affirmation/prayer: As a cell phone needs to be activated to function to it's full capacity, I too can't reach my full capacity without being activated by you Lord. Faith in You gives me the power to function above and beyond anything that I could ask or think. I open my heart to you so that I might know all the gifts, power, and possibilities that lie ahead and within me.

God is my source!

November 22

TROUBLE

Man that is born of a woman is of few days, and full of trouble.
—Job 14:1(ESV)

And the peace of God, which surpasses all understanding, will guard your hearts and your minds in Christ Jesus.
—Philippians 4:7 (ESV)

Affirmation/prayer: I will never have a trouble-free life. When trouble marches daily, ready to attack, the one weapon I have is the peace of God. True peace is not found only in the absence of trouble. True peace is found in the mist of trouble. Instead of spending this day counting the things that go wrong and having a pity party, asking, "Why me, Lord?" I will let go of worry. I will ask Jesus for solutions and his peace that is above my understanding.

God is my source!

November 23

BEING WILLING

I examined my lifestyle and set my feet in the direction of your decrees. I hurried and did not procrastinate to keep your commands.
—Psalms 119:59–60 (ISV)

Affirmation/prayer: When my day starts and ends stressfully, being willing to honestly look within may be the key to serenity.

1. Am I willing to stop trying to control things out of my control?
2. Am I willing to stop procrastinating when I can't control the outcome? ("Just do it.")
3. Am I willing to admit my mistakes?
4. Am I willing to forgive myself and others?
5. Am I willing to take care of all my physical, emotional, and spiritual needs?
6. Am I willing to do God's will and ask God for help with all of the above?

God, you are willing when I am willing. I will study your words and follow you.

God is my source!

November 24

COMMITTED

So let's not get tired of doing what is good. At just the right time we will reap a harvest of blessing if we don't give up.
—Galatians 6:9 (NLT)

Commit your actions to the LORD, and your plans will succeed.
—Proverbs 16:3 (NLT)

Affirmation/prayer: When I am committed, my actions will follow. Lord, help me to be committed to my dreams as I commit them to you. No matter what my challenges are, help me not to give up. Anchor me, Lord, and give me a heart to be committed to doing good.

God is my source!

November 25

THE THINGS I SAY

For whoever would love life and see good days must keep their tongue from evil and their lips from deceitful speech.
—1 Peter 3:10 (NIV)

So those who are smart keep their mouths shut, for it is an evil time.
—Amos 5:13 (NLT)

A time to be silent and a time to speak.
—Ecclesiastes 3:7 (NIV)

Affirmation/prayer: I alone am responsible for the words going out of my mouth. I need to be prepared for times when I will be tempted to say the wrong thing. Lord, help me guard my words. Lord, give me wisdom to know that sometimes the best thing is to say nothing at all.

God is my source!

November 26

COMFORT AND JOY

You have shown me the path to life, and you make me glad by being near to me. Sitting at your right side, I will always be joyful.
—Psalms 16:11 (CEV)

Affirmation/prayer: Thank you, Lord, for guiding me this day. Let your presence be my comfort and joy all day long.

God is my source!

November 27

MOOD SWINGS

Why are you cast down, O my soul, and why are you in turmoil within me? Hope in God; for I shall again praise him, my salvation and my God. My soul is cast down within me; therefore I remember you.
—Psalms 42:5–6 (ESV)

Hear my cry, O God, listen to my prayer; from the end of the earth I call to you when my heart is faint. Lead me to the rock that is higher than I.
—Psalms 61:1–2

Affirmation/prayer: My emotions are a gift from God that connect the soul, spirit, and body. They are my reality check of what I am believing. Faith, not moods, should guide my actions. My faith in you, Lord, is the key to keeping my emotions and moodiness under control.

Lord, give me wisdom and faith to address my imbalances—physical, mental, and spiritual. Give me peace so I may react to life by faith and not by my moods.

God is my source!

November 28

WISE OR DISHONEST FOOL

Better to be poor and honest than to be dishonest and a fool.
—Proverbs 19:1 (NLT)

Affirmation/prayer: Before I run after money or riches, help me, Lord, to decide if I am being wise or foolish.

God is my source!

November 29

THE LORD BLESS AND KEEP YOU

May the LORD bless you and protect you. May the LORD smile on you and be gracious to you. May the LORD show you his favor and give you his peace.
—Numbers 6:24–26 (NLT)

Affirmation/prayer: Amen!

God is my source!

November 30

MY HOPE

O LORD, I give my life to you.

Lead me by your truth and teach me, for you are the God who saves me. All day long I put my hope in you.
—Psalms 25:1, 5 (NLT)

Affirmation/prayer: I experience less stress and less mess when my life is in your hands, Lord. Please lead me by your truth and teach me. All day long I put my hope in You.

God is my source!

December

December 1

CHRONIC COMPLAINER

Peace I leave with you; my peace I give you. I do not give to you as the world gives. Do not let your hearts be troubled and do not be afraid.
—John 14:27 (NIV)

Affirmation/prayer: Jesus, even in the midst of trials, give me peace to not upset my environment by being a chronic complainer. Please remove all my fears and doubts. Lord, I pray for the peace to do your will, be it to accept, change, or move on.

God is my source!

December 2

HOLD YOUR HEAD UP

For he will conceal me there when troubles come; he will hide me in his sanctuary. He will place me out of reach on a high rock. Then my head will be held high above my enemies around me.

Wait for the LORD; be strong and take heart and wait for the LORD.
—Psalms 27:5–6, 14 (NLT)

Set your minds on things above, not on earthly things.
—Colossians 3:2 (NIV)

Affirmation/prayer: Instead of holding my head down because of the negativity around me, I will look up, pray, and seek his goodness. I have confidence in all my affairs that God is a good God. As long as I live, I will be strong and wait on God. I will hold my head up.

God is my source!

December 3

TO THINE OWN SELF BE TRUE

Who can understand the human heart? There is nothing else so deceitful; it is too sick to be healed. I, the LORD, search the minds and test the hearts of people. I treat each of them according to the way they live, according to what they do.
—Jeremiah 17:9–10 (GNT)

Affirmation/prayer: I will take the time to examine my ways and truths. I will not deceive myself, even if the person I see cause me pain. Lord, I need you to repair any deceitful, sick, or weak parts so that I may be healed. Replace any damaged part with courage, strength, and love. Make it a heart that bears good fruit.

God is my source!

December 4

WISDOM BRINGS HAPPINESS

Happy is anyone who becomes wise—who comes to have understanding.

Wisdom can make your life pleasant and lead you safely through it. Those who become wise are happy; wisdom will give them life.
—Proverbs 3:13, 17–18 (GNT)

Affirmation/prayer: Lord, before I act or speak today, help me be wise and get a good understanding. Being wise will guide me to peace and happiness.

God is my source!

December 5

LOVE

If I gave everything I have to the poor and even sacrificed my body, I could boast about it; but if I didn't love others, I would have gained nothing. Love is patient and kind. Love is not jealous or boastful or proud or rude. It does not demand its own way. It is not irritable, and it keeps no record of being wronged. It does not rejoice about injustice but rejoices whenever the truth wins out. Love never gives up, never loses faith, is always hopeful, and endures through every circumstance.
—1 Corinthians 13:3–7 (NLT)

Affirmation/prayer: Lord, help me to remember to love before I act or speak. Love helps me treat others with patience and kindness. Love means never giving up or losing hope. Thank you, Jesus, for your gift of love. Without love, I am nothing.

God is my source!

December 6

DON'T GIVE UP

And I am convinced that nothing can ever separate us from God's love. Neither death nor life, neither angels nor demons, neither our fears for today nor our worries about tomorrow—not even the powers of hell can separate us from God's love.
—Romans 8:38 (NLT)

Affirmation/prayer: Life can be rough. Fears try to stop me. Worry says you can't go on. Messages from Satan try to tell me that it is no use just give up. However, your word tells me that you have never left me and never will. Now I fight on, and I will never, never give up.

God is my source!

December 7

GOD IS ALL I NEED

Abba	Father	*Romans 8:15*
Elohim	The Creator	*Genesis 1:1*
Yahweh-Raah	The LORD My Shepherd	*Psalms 23:1*
Yahweh-Jireh	The LORD Will Provide	*Genesis 22:11–14*
Yahweh-Rapha	The LORD That Healeth	*Exodus 15:26*
Yahweh-Shalom	The LORD Is Peace	*Psalms 29:11*
El Roi	The God Who Sees	*Genesis 16:13*
El Deah	The God of Knowledge	*1 Samuel 2:3*
El Olam	The Everlasting God	*Psalms 72:17,19*
Alpha and Omega	The Beginning and the End	*Revelation 1:8*
Jesus Christ	My Lord and Savior	*John 20:30–31*

Affirmation/prayer: In God, I can find everything I need.

God is my source!

December 8

FAITH

Faith shows the reality of what we hope for; it is the evidence of things we cannot see.
—Hebrews 11:1 (NLT)

For we live by believing and not by seeing.
—2 Corinthians 5:7 (NLT)

Affirmation/prayer: I will continue to pursue my dreams in spite of the forces that come against me. Even when I do not see my situations changing, I will keep the faith knowing that God loves me I will pray and put my will, my reality, my future, and my hope in God.

God is my source!

December 9

YOU CAN'T PRAY A LIE

Behold, You desire truth in the innermost being, And in the hidden part You will make me know wisdom.
—Psalms 51:6 (NASB)

Affirmation/prayer: Lord, when I am honest and not making excuses for my behaviors, it opens my heart to receive your grace and wisdom. There is no sin you can't remove. There are no problems I can't solve with your wisdom. You already know my heart (Prov. 21:2). Help me to take an honest look within. No more lies or excuses, but changes in behavior from deep within is what I seek. Thank you for your love, mercy, and wisdom.

God is my source!

December 10

TRUST IN THE LORD

Fearing people is a dangerous trap, but trusting the LORD means safety.
—Proverbs 29:25

No eye has seen, no ear has heard, and no mind has imagined what God has prepared for those who love him.
—1 Corinthians 2:9 (NLT)

Affirmation/prayer: Lord, restore in me any self-respect or hope lost from trying to be what everyone else says I should be. My unfulfilled spirit comes from not listening to your spirit within. Thank you for being my hope of good things to come. I will love and trust you above all.

God is my source!

December 11

IT'S IN HIS HANDS

But ask the animals, and they will teach you, or the birds in the sky, and they will tell you; Or speak to the earth, and it will teach you, or let the fish in the sea inform you.

In his hand is the life of every creature and the breath of all mankind.
—Job 12:7–8, 10 (NIV)

Affirmation/prayer: No matter what I encounter this week, good or bad, I will remember this: it's in his hands.

God is my source!

December 12

SWEET COMMUNICATION

LORD, who may dwell in your sacred tent? Who may live on your holy mountain? The one whose walk is blameless, who does what is righteous, who speaks the truth from their heart.
—Psalms 15:1–2 (NIV)

Affirmation/prayer: Jesus, please give me the courage to take an honest look within. Change only happens when I acknowledge the things I need to change. If I refuse to speak in truth in prayer, communication with you fails. Give me the courage to pray honestly, speak honestly, walk in integrity, and do the right things. Lord, thank you for loving me and giving me the opportunity to have sweet communication with you.

God is my source!

December 13

PERFECT IN WEAKNESS

Each time he said, "My grace is all you need. My power works best in weakness." So now I am glad to boast about my weaknesses, so that the power of Christ can work through me.
—2 Corinthians 12:9 (NLT)

Affirmation/prayer: When I am at my lowest and weakest point, that is where God is most powerful in my life. Instead of complaining today about what I am going through, I will tell others that I am still standing because God's grace and power has brought me through. When I am fearful and don't know what to do, please remind me, Jesus, that your power is made perfect when I am at my weakest.

God is my source!

December 14

STEADFAST LOVE

Remember your mercy, O LORD, and your steadfast love, for they have been from of old. Remember not the sins of my youth or my transgressions; according to your steadfast love remember me, for the sake of your goodness, O LORD!
—Psalms 25:6–7 (EST)

Affirmation/prayer: The Lord is indeed merciful and extends his steadfast love to me daily. Thank you for a constant love in spite of my weaknesses, a love that lifts me up and instructs me in the way to go.

God is my source!

December 15

DENIAL AND TRUTH

The LORD is near to all who call on him, to all who call on him in truth.
—Psalms 145:18 (NIV)

But when he, the Spirit of truth, comes, he will guide you into all the truth. He will not speak on his own; he will speak only what he hears, and he will tell you what is yet to come.
—John 16:13 (NIV)

Affirmation/prayer: Truth, not denial, is my friend. Truth helps me face the pains of life so that I can move forward. Jesus, you are the truth (John 14:6). Please let your love softly strengthen me. Please lead me away from living in denial about my circumstances, into a life of truth, joy, and peace.

God is my source!

December 16

FEELING UNAPPRECIATED

May the LORD repay you for what you have done. May you be richly rewarded by the LORD, the God of Israel, under whose wings you have come to take refuge.
—Ruth 2:12 (NIV)

This is what the LORD says: "Restrain your voice from weeping and your eyes from tears, for your work will be rewarded," declares the LORD….
—Jeremiah 31:16 (NIV)

Let us not become weary in doing good, for at the proper time we will reap a harvest if we do not give up.
—Galatians 6:9 (NIV)

Affirmation/prayer: When I give so much, and no one seems to appreciate the good that I do. When I do not even get a thank-you because this world sees my good as just another thing required of me. When Satan tries to turn my good for bad as he stirs up envy, jealousy, and lies among those whom I would serve. I will thank God, who sees the good I do. He tells me not to fret and relax. I can rejoice because he is rewarding my good deedshere on earth and in the life to come.

God is my source!

December 17

REMINDER

The LORD is my light and my salvation; whom shall, I fear? The LORD is the stronghold of my life; of whom shall I be afraid?
—Psalms 27:1 (NIV)

When the angel of the LORD appeared to Gideon, he said, "The LORD is with you, mighty warrior."
—Judges 6:12 (NIV)

Affirmation/prayer: Lord, please do not let me forget your mighty power that you give me because you love me. I will put my fears aside and trust in God. In you, I am a mighty warrior.

God is my source!

December 18

PROSPERITY

Beloved, I pray that in every way you may prosper and enjoy good health, as your soul also prospers.
—3 John 1:2 (KJV)

Affirmation/prayer: Lord, I need you. Renew me physically, emotionally, and spiritually. Prosper me inward and out, so I may do good deeds and be of service to you and others. As you give me good things, I am filled with peace, happiness, and joy! Amen.

God is my source!

December 19

HE SEES AND LISTENS

LORD, the God of Israel, enthroned between the cherubim, you alone are God over all the kingdoms of the earth. You have made heaven and earth. Bend down, O LORD, and listen! Open your eyes, O LORD, and see!
—2 Kings 19:15–16 (NIV)

Affirmation/prayer: Lord, some days I feel that you are so far away from me. On those days your word reminds that you see everything. You see my circumstances and hear my prayers. In your name, victory is mine.

God is my source!

December 20

BLESS THE LORD, O MY SOUL

Bless the LORD, O my soul, and all that is within me, bless his holy name! Praise the LORD, my soul, and forget not all his benefits.
—Psalms 103:1–2 (ESV)

Affirmation/prayer: As another week comes to a close, I will take the time to praise God. He has seen me through the rain. His hand has healed me, uplifted me, forgiven me, and satisfied all my needs.

Bless the Lord, O my soul, and forget not all his benefits!

God is my source!

December 21

JUST ONE SMILE

The LORD bless you and protect you. May the LORD smile on you and be gracious to you. May the LORD show you his favor and give you his peace.
—Numbers 6:24–26 (NLT)

Affirmation/prayer: Just one smile from God, and I have all the protection, grace, favor, and peace I need. Lord, please bless and smile on me.

God is my source!

December 22

YOU WILL BE BLESSED

The LORD will make your businesses and your farms successful.

You will have plenty of bread to eat. The LORD will make you successful in your daily work. The LORD will help you defeat your enemies and make them scatter in all directions.

If you follow and obey the LORD, he will make you his own special people, just as he promised.
—Deuteronomy 28:3, 5–7, 9 (CEV)

Affirmation/prayer: As a child of God through Jesus, I can have all these promises and more. Even when trouble rises, he will protect me and see me through. Jesus, give me grace and strength to follow and stay in your will for my life. Thank you for your awesome blessings.

God is my source!

December 23

NEVER ALONE

I will walk among you and be your God, and you will be my people.
—Leviticus 26:12 (NIV)

I pray that out of his glorious riches he may strengthen you with power through his Spirit in your inner being.
—Ephesians 3:16 (NIV)

Affirmation/prayer: Praise you, Lord, that I don't have to walk this life alone. You are always with me. I just need to tap into the Holy Spirit within me to feel Your presence, strength, and power.

God is my source!

December 24

HE IS ABLE

May God give you more and more mercy, peace, and love.

Now all glory to God, who is able to keep you from falling away and will bring you with great joy into his glorious presence without a single fault.
—Jude 1:2, 24 (NLT)

Affirmation/prayer: I have peace and mercy and joy in my heart knowing that I have a God who is able to keep me in the faith, even though I sometimes make mistakes. Thank you, Jesus, for forgiving and loving me.

God is my source!

December 25

TRUE LOVE

Love means doing what God has commanded us, and he has commanded us to love one another, just as you heard from the beginning.
—2 John 1:6 (NLT)

If you love me, obey my commandments.
—John 14:15 (NLT)

Affirmation/prayer: Saying I love you is easy. True love for God and others will be seen in my actions. May my love actions speak louder than my words. Lord, help me love you more than this world. Surround me with your loving arms so I may obey you and follow your lead.

God is my source!

December 26

THE GIFT THAT KEEPS ON GIVING

"Bring the whole tithe into the storehouse, that there may be food in my house. Test me in this," says the LORD Almighty, "and see if I will not throw open the floodgates of heaven and pour out so much blessing that there will not be room enough to store it."
—Malachi 3:10 (NIV)

For where your treasure is, there your heart will be also.
—Matthew 6:21 (NIV)

Affirmation/prayer: Lord, although I am not under the old law, I will not forget to return a portion of my blessings to you. When you examine my heart, may I be found faithful in all areas of my life. May my heart be first for you. For my heart will be with the things I treasure most. Thank you for loving me. Jesus, you are the gift that keeps on giving.

God is my source!

December 27

HIS LOVE CALMS ME

For the LORD your God is living among you. He is a mighty savior. He will take delight in you with gladness. With his love, he will calm all your fears. He will rejoice over you with joyful songs.
—Zephaniah 3:17 (NLT)

For God has said, "I will never fail you. I will never abandon you."
—Hebrews 13:5

Affirmation/prayer: Today, Lord Jesus, there have been and will be times when life seems uncertain. During these times I have peace because your love calms all my fears. It is you who puts joy in my heart even during my difficult moments. It is good to know a loving Savior who rejoices over me and calms me because I am his child. Thank you for never leaving or forsaking me.

God is my source!

December 28

BRIGHT, SHINING STAR

Those who are wise will shine like the brightness of the heavens, and those who lead many to righteousness, like the stars for ever and ever.
—Daniel 12:3 (NIV)

Then the righteous will shine like the sun in the kingdom of their Father. Whoever has ears, let them hear.
—Matthew 13:43 (NIV)

Affirmation/prayer: Jesus, thank you for saving me and rescuing me from a world of darkness. Help me shine like the stars at night and the sun during the day. I need your courage and strength to be a shining star for those that I may meet. As light illuminates the darkness, may my actions and speech shine bright, no matter what circumstances that I encounter. Give me the wisdom and courage to share the gospel, leading others to Christ so they will carry your light that illuminates this dark world. God is my shining star.

God is my source!

December 29

A NEW HEART

Create in me a pure heart, O God, and renew a steadfast spirit within me.
—Psalms 51:10 (NIV)

I will give you a new heart and put a new spirit in you; I will remove from you your heart of stone and give you a heart of flesh.
—Ezekiel 36:26 (NIV)

Therefore, if anyone is in Christ, the new creation has come: The old has gone, the new is here!
—2 Corinthians 5:17 (NIV)

Affirmation/prayer: Jesus, I am so glad that I am your child. Thank You, that I am a new creation. You erased my past heartaches and puts joy in my heart. My new heart is no longer ashamed of past mistakes. My heart tells me that I am loved by Jesus. My heart sings praises to God, knowing that one day I will be with him forever.

God is my source!

December 30

FORGIVING AN OFFENSE

Never take your own revenge, beloved, but leave room for the wrath of God, for it is written, "VENGEANCE IS MINE, I WILL REPAY," says the Lord.
—Romans 12:19 (NASB)

Do not gloat over your brother's day, The day of his misfortune…
—Obadiah 1:12 (NASB)

Then Peter came and said to Him, "Lord, how often shall my brother sin against me and I forgive him? Up to seven times?" Jesus said to him, "I do not say to you, up to seven times, but up to seventy times seven.
—Matthew 18:21–22 (NASB)

Affirmation/prayer: Lord, you know how it feels to be brokenhearted as the result of the actions of others. When I act out of ego and pride, getting revenge will be my first go-to. Jesus, you are a loving and forgiving God. Teach me how to set healthy boundaries when it comes to dealing with those who would do me wrong. Help me forgive and forget any offenses that may have occurred in my past. Teach me how to love and forgive those who offend.

God is my source!

December 31

DO NOT LIVE IN FEAR

Don't be afraid. I am with you. Don't tremble with fear. I am your God. I will make you strong, as I protect you with my arm and give you victories.
—Isaiah 41:10 (CEV)

Our LORD and our God, you are like the sun and also like a shield. You treat us with kindness and with honor, never denying any good thing to those who live right.
—Psalms 84:11

Our LORD, you bless those who live right, and you shield them with your kindness.
—Psalms 5:12 (CEV)

Affirmation/prayer: I know that the spirit of fear is not from God. Yet I let it rule my life on many occasions. The opportunities that I have missed were often missed because I will too afraid to try, too afraid of failure or what others may say. Jesus, let me feel your shield of faith that surrounds me when I am afraid. Give me the courage to live life in spite of my fears. Give me the courage to go forth and receive all of the good things you have waiting for your children.

God is my source!

My Story of how I became a Christian

ACKNOWLEDGEMENTS

DEDICATION

DAILY WISDOM

My Story of How I Became a Christian.

I heard the gospel message. Someone told me about the gospel (good news) how Christ died for my sins. (1 Cor. 15:1–4). I actually listened.
So, faith comes from hearing, that is, hearing the Good News about Christ.
—Romans 10:17 (NLT)

I believed the Good News. (Faith): Heb. 11:6). *And it is impossible to please God without faith. Anyone who wants to come to him must believe that God exists and that he rewards those who sincerely seek him* (NLT).

I decided I wanted to live a better life. I repented of my sins. *If we say we have not sinned, we are fooling ourselves, and the truth isn't in our hearts. But if we confess our sins to God, he will keep his promise and do what is right: he will forgive us our sins and purify us from all our wrongdoing.*
—1 John 1:8–9 (NLT)

I confessed that *Jesus is the son of God* (1 John 4:15). Whoever confesses that Jesus is the son of God, God abides in him, and he in God.

I asked to be baptized (Rom. 6:4). We were therefore buried with him through baptism into death in order that, just as Christ was raised from the dead through the glory of the Father, we, too, may live new lives.

It took courage for me to tell my story. I hope my story will give you the courage to share the gospel with someone else. I hope that if you have not considered being a Christian, this is the day that you will give it some thought. I believe that the whole Bible, from Genesis to Revelation, and its message, is about a God that sees *you* and truly loves *you*.

Now to Him who is able to keep you from stumbling, And to present you faultless Before the presence of His glory with exceeding joy, God our Savior, who alone is wise Be glory and majesty, Dominion and power, Both now and forever.
—Jude 1:24–25

Acknowledgments

First and foremost, I would like to thank God and the Holy Spirit, the true authors of this book. Daily I looked to the Bible and the Holy Spirit to guide me as I sent the many text messages to those who were inspired, encouraged, and uplifted through applying scriptures to everyday life. Without the strength that I found in God and his word this book would not have been written.

I would like to thank my sons, Christopher and Adam Murphy, who are my inspiration for writing this book. The many inspirational videos, texts, and thumbs-up sent to me helped me see this project from start to finish. Truly they are wise beyond their years. I would like to thank my daughter-in-law Tammy Murphy, who was able to see how unique this book would be among the many other meditation books. She said, "Granny, there are a lot of meditation books, but there are a lot of people who need them."

I am also especially thankful to Earl Jones, my brother, who has been my biggest supporter. Thanks go out to my friend Jamie Rayford. She has been a faithful friend who often used the phrase "God is my source." I have held on to this phrase, and it has gotten me through hard times and the writing of this book.

Thanks to my friends Mary Lyons and Crichelle, who have always been constant listeners and encouragers in my life since our college days.

Thanks to my friends Gary Henderson, Sherrian Morgan and Lula Morris, authors themselves, whose advice me as well as pointed me to much-needed resources in writing my first book, *Truly, God Is My Source.*

Thanks to the editors and publishers of Palmetto Publishing Group for publishing this book

Dedication

TO MY GRANDCHILDREN

Chasedi L.

> *Solid Rock*
> *"Anyone who listens to my teaching and follows it is*
> *wise, like a person who builds a house on solid rock.*
> *Matthew 7:24*

To: Chasedi, Dallas, Christian and future grandchildren,
I hope that this book will be a source of hope, peace, joy and
love in the years to come.

Love: Granny Murphy
A.K.A. by you as – Granny with The Peppermint.

Daily Wisdom

February

February

March

March

April

May

June

June

June

July

July

September

1.	I Am Willing	John 5:5–6 Phil. 4:13
2.	Tribulations	Hebrews 10:23
3.	A Thankful Heart	Psalms 103:2–5
4.	Cloud Coverage	Isaiah 25:5
5.	He Gives Me Joy	Romans 15:13, 1 Peter 1:8–9
6.	The True Vine	John 15:5
7.	Amazing Grace	Acts 20:32. 1 Peter 5:10
8.	Praise	Psalms 103:2, 1 Chronicles 16:34, Psalms 113:3
9.	My Friend	2 Samuel 22:32–33 John 15:15
10.	Deep Waters	2 Samuel 22:17, 20
11.	Well Done	Hebrews 6:10
12.	Flourishing like an Olive Tree	Psalms 52:8
13.	Learning to Wait on God	Psalms 27:14, Psalms 25:5
14.	Need, Not Greed	1 John 5:14
15.	Seek My Face	Psalms 27:8
16.	First Things First	Matthew 6:31–33
17.	Yet I Will Rejoice	Habakkuk 3:17–19
18.	Change	Ephesians 4:22–23 John 5:8

September

October

November

November

December

About the Author

Sandra Murphy who lives in Houston, Texas enjoys spending time with her two sons and their families. She enjoyed working many years in cancer research before she decided to pursued her true passion which is teaching. She has now retired from teaching in the public classroom. She says that her greatest joy is teaching bible classes in her local congregations. Her love for God's word and the many years of developing lessons for these bible classes has been most instrumental in writing "Truly God Is My Source". She says that her life experiences and those of the young women in her community which she mentors inspired her to address some of today's life trials in the light of God's word. She hopes that writing "Truly, God Is My Source" will serve as an example to her family, friends and those she mentors that it is never too late to follow your dreams. Most of all she prays that her life serves as an example that it is never too late to share God's love, and the saving grace of Jesus Christ.

Notes

_____

_____

_____

_____

_____

_____

_____

_____

_____

_____

_____

_____

_____

_____

_____

_____

_____

_____

_____

Notes

_____

_____

_____

_____

_____

_____

_____

_____

_____

_____

_____

_____

_____

_____

_____

_____

_____